# PRINCIPLES
## *of the*
# AMERICAN
# REPUBLIC

## DAN SCHWARTZ

ISBN 978-0-615-38843-4
Library of Congress Control Number: 2010910589

*This essay is dedicated to America's early leaders. Without their courage, intellect, and integrity, the nation in which we live today would not exist.*

# CONTENTS

# ACKNOWLEDGMENTS

I wish to thank all those who assisted with writing this essay over the past four decades: family, friends, teachers, editors, and many others who provided comments, the inspiration to learn, and the time and space to think and write. In particular, I would like to thank Richard Beeman and Brannon Denning for their insightful comments; Kristi Hein, for her thoughtful editing; and Yanan, for her smiling support.

Dan Schwartz
January 2012

# I. PRINCIPLES OF THE AMERICAN REPUBLIC

The Constitution has been subject to interpretation since the day it was signed in September 1787. This essay offers once such interpretation, premised on the belief that the Constitution is a blueprint for American society and that it incorporates basic principles aimed at creating a foundation for the country as it existed then and to settle the inevitable conflicts that would arise in the future.

The men who wrote the Constitution designed a government aimed at resolving divergent sectional and commercial interests. It was never intended as purely a legal document or one that would remain static over time. The fifteen principles reflect how political authority should be allocated, how the economy should be organized, how the legal system should operate, and how American society should function. Some of the principles are in conflict with others; other principles can be interpreted in different ways. Some principles loom larger than others, but all are relevant. This essay describes that structure: identifying the principles, describing their evolution over two centuries, and looking at how these changes have impacted our government in 2012.

\* \* \* \* \*

At one time or another, we have all asked ourselves a simple question: what will become of America? Will our fate be that of Egypt or Rome: vast civilizations whose scattered ruins are the only remains of past glory? Or that of the political states of Europe, whose empires have long since faded? Will we be like China, a civilization that constantly reinvents itself? Or will we become something different?

Most of us believe that the country's early leaders intended something new, a clean break from the aristocratic past they defeated in the Revolution. That is why the Constitution is an extraordinary document: a model for government, built on compromise and experience, yet founded on a set of principles that project how, ideally, government and society should act.

In post-revolutionary America, growing economic uncertainty and a failing political system alarmed the country's early leaders. In James Madison's words, "[No] money comes into the public treasury, trade is on a wretched footing, and the states are running mad after paper money."[1] The postwar depression that hit the colonies in 1783 bottomed in the summer of 1786. Because the national government had no authority to tax, the Continental Congress had amassed ever larger foreign and domestic debts. In addition, a uniform and stable currency had not yet been established. Increasingly worthless paper money flooded the states.

In September 1786, motivated by economic necessity and political reality, the state of Virginia called a conference in Annapolis to address these concerns. It was formally entitled "Meeting of Commissioners to Remedy Defects of the Federal Government," and delegates from only five states attended. Those present realized that resolving these problems was beyond their brief. They sent a letter to the Continental Congress proposing a more ambitious gathering.

During the winter of 1786–87, two thousand farmers in Western

Massachusetts rose in armed rebellion under Daniel Shays, a Revolutionary War veteran. The local militia easily put down the uprising, but other states had their own poor areas and unhappy debtors. News of the conflict hastened the decision by all states except Rhode Island to send delegates to the Constitutional Convention in Philadelphia in May 1787. United by their recent victory in the fight for independence and their desire to "form a more perfect union," many of the country's early leaders met at the Convention to debate their differences and to try to settle them.

Madison's *Notes to the Convention* emphasized that a crumbling economic order was a prime motivator for the Constitutional Convention. The public debt "remained without any provision for its payment"; the "want of a general power over Commerce, led to an exercise of the power separately, by the States"; and "a general decay of confidence & credit" left the delegates with few options. As the states increasingly refused to cooperate with the national government, wrote Madison, "the condition of the U.S. could not but fill the public mind with gloom."[2]

The early leaders who convened in Philadelphia shared beliefs inspired by the era's foremost thinkers and shaped by their own experience. These ideals were cast into a unified set of principles, setting the foundation for their ultimate achievement: the United States Constitution. Inherently a legal document, the Constitution's foundations rest equally on political, economic, and social principles.

The Convention delegates spent most of their time discussing what the new government could and could not do and sorting out responsibilities among its different branches and among the former colonies. They searched for a basis on which sectional interests could participate fairly in government.

The Constitution reflects the political theory of its authors, a social contract that holds that "governments derive their just powers from the consent of the governed."³ In designing this compact between citizens and their elected officials, the authors of the Constitution had choices to make but few examples to follow: England offered Parliament, but the king held too many of the cards. The delegates were also familiar with the colonial assemblies and Continental Congress. These institutions served their purpose but did not meet the new country's expanded needs.

The Framers considered these precedents and designed a new system, "a fabric without model." Other countries' governments were founded on the aggregation of authority; the Framers took the opposite approach. They divided authority in order to control it. Concerned about both the abuse and the concentration of power, as well as the government's ability to achieve its objectives, they parceled out the authority derived from a single source—the people—among multiple branches and levels. Their "checks and balances" operated internally, through separation of powers among three branches, and vertically, though a federal structure. They created national and state levels of government and partitioned legislative, executive, and judicial authority within each level.

The Convention delegates worried about the qualifications of those who would occupy elected office. They established an electoral process that insulated the government from direct representation by class and by moneyed and sectional interests. They hoped the system would promote experienced and virtuous leaders to public office—because the delegates realized that no matter how carefully they balanced competing interests within the constitutional framework, their ultimate success depended on the individuals chosen to lead the new republic. William Penn wrote in the early 1700s, "[G]overnments, like clocks, go from the motion men give them, and as governments are made and moved by men, so by them they are ruined too."⁴

George Washington and his fellow delegates also recognized that economic prosperity was a precondition to political stability, and that, in turn, political stability was essential to economic progress. The Constitutional Convention envisioned a commercial system founded on free trade *and* a level playing field. To ensure that everyone had an equal chance, the government would act as a referee, stepping in when necessary to settle disputes and address inequities and unfair advantages. Government would enforce private contracts and intervene in the markets only when necessary.

The Framers drew upon their English common-law heritage and adopted an adversary system of justice, the legal equivalent of the "every man for himself" model of open markets and free trade. They incorporated the individual's right to chart his own destiny and to influence that of others, subject to the limits of our legal system.

The Constitution also reflected important social values. The delegates intended their new country to be a pluralistic society that respected human dignity and accommodated different cultural values—a society that afforded infinite second chances and the opportunity to earn unprecedented wealth for those willing to stay late and take risks. In America's "can do" society, "You made a mistake? So what? Try again!" provides the chorus for those who have stumbled. And the Constitution promoted an equalitarian society. "Our greatest goal is to give the average family the opportunity to earn an income, to own a home, to educate their children, and to have some security in their later years," said former Speaker of the House Tip O'Neill. "I believe it is wrong for the people who made it up the ladder to pull the ladder up behind them. This is an alien philosophy. We Americans believe in hard work, in getting ahead, but we also believe in looking out for the other guy."[5] In an equalitarian society, winning isn't everything or the only thing—but *how* you play the game that matters most.

The Framers protected multiple points of view and encouraged the formation of associations and groups. They separated church and state and further reinforced the foundations of an open society that respected individual beliefs and religious freedom.

The final principle (some say the first) is national security: government's obligation to protect its citizens at home and abroad from those who would undermine our way of life. The principle of national security advances our national interest. This national interest is aimed at protecting our citizens' welfare, and, uniquely among nations, America has sought to promote its core values of political liberty and economic opportunity.

Incredibly, the most revolutionary doctrine in history was written by a group of prosperous and educated men who cared deeply about the country they were creating. The Constitution embodies the delegates' efforts to disaggregate and distribute decision-making authority by creating multiple centers of authority and by defining the limits of what government could and could not do. Throughout all the turmoil inherent in a system founded on competing centers of authority, the delegates hoped to protect liberty and promote equality. They believed that a political equilibrium would result, welding the colony's diverse interests into a coherent nation and effective government. Their ideals married the colonists' basic aspirations for a democratic and free society to their experience with representative government. And throughout the 220 years that followed, Americans have worked to make this union a success.

\* \* \* \* \*

The Constitutional Convention designed a novel mechanism to manage the country's many sectional and commercial interests. There were and remain many competing values and objectives in the Constitution, but the tension between liberty and equality is the most salient. Maintaining a balance between them lies at the heart of two great challenges the country has faced: ending slavery and alleviating poverty.

Liberty is the hallmark of American society. It takes several forms: political freedom, through protections found in the Constitution and Bill of Rights; legal freedom, through guarantees and other rights the courts have established; economic freedom, through fair competition and limited government intervention; and social freedom, through pluralism and religious tolerance.

The Convention delegates never believed that all men were created totally equal. But the country's abundant land and natural resources reinforced the social and economic equality that the Constitution sought to protect. The colonists' fight for political liberty would have been to no avail if the yeoman farmer went hungry or had to pitch his tent on the Commons. In the words of America's first sociologist, Alexis de Tocqueville, "[E]quality of condition is the fundamental fact from which all others seem to be derived."

Equality sets boundaries on liberty. Liberty secures individual autonomy and freedom from government interference; equality, at the very least, demands similar opportunities for all and elevates the common good over individual demands.

America's early leaders tried hard to gauge the challenges their new republic would face. The delegates focused on the distribution of political authority: among the three branches of government and between the state and national governments. They did their best to balance liberty and equality but left the boundaries unmarked. Proclaiming that "all men are created equal," the Declaration of Independence also affirms "that they are endowed by their Creator with certain unalienable Rights, that among these are Life, Liberty and the pursuit of Happiness." Seventy-five years later, the boundaries were clearer but still uncertain. At Gettysburg, Abraham Lincoln spoke of both "a nation conceived in liberty and dedicated to the proposition that all men are created equal."[6]

Of course, for well over two centuries, liberty and equality largely excluded blacks, women, religious and ethnic minorities.

Those who drafted the Constitution intuitively believed that liberty and equality could coexist once virtuous leaders put their hearts and minds together. In fact, establishing equilibrium between the two has been the fulcrum of America's political system. Today, this task remains no less important—or difficult.

If nothing else, the principles articulate a worthy starting point for renewing our government's ability to make decisions and to deliver the democracy we have promised ourselves.

\*   \*   \*   \*   \*

History and law professors and their daily world counterparts have done a superb job of writing about the Constitution's history and exploring its deeper meanings. By and large, though, they have not expanded their insights to consider a broader interpretation of the Constitution beyond separate political, legal, economic, or social perspectives; nor have they looked at the implications of what they have written about the Constitution for how our country has changed over its history.

Richard Beeman, a professor of history at the University of Pennsylvania and author of several books on the Constitution, suggested that this book pay "more attention to that area in which some of those fifteen principles sometimes find themselves in conflict with, or at least tension with, some of the others. Moreover, the source of many of our constitutional controversies is not so much that we possess different principles, but that some of us give greater weight to some of those principles than others." Finally, he adds, the "original meaning of some of those principles, e.g., federalism and separation of powers, is not at all self-evident, or generally agreed upon, even by the men who created the Constitution."[7]

Professor Beeman is quite correct on all three points. Several principles are, in fact, in conflict with one another: liberty and equality, free markets and government intervention, individual selfishness and public virtue, national supremacy and local efficiency—the list goes on.

Although the Constitution does not solve the conflict, it does provide a political framework in which to balance these competing values and objectives. The Framers did spend more time on certain principles, such as federalism and separation of powers. But to miss the other principles—such as judicial review, free markets, or pluralism—is to reduce the Constitution to merely a legal document. The several political, economic, legal, and social principles play an equally important role.

What do the principles mean? Are "we the people" or "we the states" the final repository of government legitimacy and authority? Which rights does the Constitution guarantee, and which rights are discretionary? How do we perpetuate public virtue in public officials? Where is the distinction between "judicial review" and "judicial activism"? Where do we draw the line between government assistance and government intervention in free markets? How do we balance liberty and equality? The answers are not at all clear.

Americans, though, must finally decide what the Constitution means. Ostensibly, that is the Supreme Court's role, but the nine justices are not disinterested bystanders. The Convention never resolved the issue of slavery—grossly incompatible with the ideals of the Revolution, but intractable when it came to forming a national government. The Supreme Court did not decide it either. Seventy years later, at the cost of 620,000 American lives, we came to a decision in the Civil War: equality of opportunity means exactly that. It then took another century for that meaning to become a reality.

Today, we face another dilemma: the inequality between different economic strata. No society in history has been able to eliminate the difference between social classes. Yet no society has survived a permanent chasm between rich and poor. It is testament to the strength of our democracy that we can freely debate this question.

Beyond Professor Beeman's observations that tension exists among the principles, that some are more important than others, that we disagree on their meaning, over the past sixty years, the principles themselves have become marginalized. We have lost the ability to make decisions necessary to thoughtfully govern ourselves.

\* \* \* \* \*

The constitutional balancing mechanism operated through principles that were built into the document itself. Most are clear from the text; others can be directly inferred from the wording or the papers and letters written by those who attended the Convention. These principles assert the political, legal, economic, and social means by which the Convention delegates achieved their desired results. (*Sources of the Principles*, at the end of this section, details the principles' origins in the Constitution.)

Political principles address the underlying legitimacy of government: its purpose, role, and structure. There are five *political principles*: (1) social contract, (2) natural rights, (3) federalism, (4) restraints on a single source of political authority, and (5) public virtue.

The Constitution is a legal document, both in itself and in the judicial system it mandates. It includes four *legal principles*: (6)

common law, (7) judicial review, (8) adversary system of criminal justice, and (9) private ordering. Economic principles ultimately frame the economic ends of government. There are two *economic principles*: (10) direct but limited government involvement in the economy and (11) free trade (free markets).

The Constitution rests equally on values reflected in the social conditions and ideals that existed in early America. There are three *social principles*: (12) pluralism, (13) equalitarian society, and (14) separation of church and state. The final principle is (15) *national security*.

## POLITICAL PRINCIPLES

Political principles address the underlying legitimacy of government: its purpose, role, and structure. Each political principle has its own history, but over time the political principles have largely lost their meaning. The protections and safeguards that the original system created no longer exist. We the people have to decide whether the government we have is the government we want.

## SOCIAL CONTRACT

The principle that democratic government derives its legitimacy from the consent of the governed was implicit in the very act of creating a written constitution. It addresses both the source and the scope of government power. This principle rests on the belief that elected officials govern with the permission and participation of the governed. The growth, size, and complexity of modern government have never replaced this integral component of representative democracy.

Social contract provides the basis of our government, but as a principle it has been largely forgotten. "Consent of the governed" has become "permission of the few."

The principle of social contract lies at the heart of debates over redistricting and gerrymandering. Widespread gerrymandering is a relatively recent phenomenon. With fewer and fewer congressional candidates facing opposition, political power has been handed to those small numbers behind the majority party candidate. The victor in the primary takes the November election as well, usually winning in the primary with 10 percent or less of the district's total population. Of course, the larger issue is, why do we have districts dominated by one party or the other? The answer, in far too many cases: pointed redistricting to achieve one-party dominance, founded on the tacit agreement between the parties to relinquish one district in exchange for controlling another.

The principle of social contract is also behind the ongoing dispute over lobbyists and political appointments. The issue with "pay-to-play" or cronyism is that it short-circuits the decision-making process. That is, elected officials will accord special interests a privileged position rather than weighing what's best for those who elected them. In many instances, elected officials speak with the same voice (literally, the same words) as those representing industry.[8] Party discipline, business benefits for contributors, and political posturing have replaced responses to the very real needs the country faces: education, infrastructure, jobs, and more. Refusing to cut costs that might alienate large interest groups has stood in the way of taking necessary steps to fiscal responsibility. Partisanship and self-interest have replaced principled decision making to reach a particular end.

The "glue of compromise" that has held the country together has become unhinged.

Solutions to the vanishing principle of social contract are not hard to find. We can curtail campaign spending and encourage more Americans to run for office. We can encourage the electorate to spend time on the workings of their government rather than on celebrity gossip. Supreme Court opinions aside, there must be limits to campaign spending. Freedom of speech must be weighed against the ends of democratic government. The ability to spend one's own money negates the advantage of entrenched officials, but the question of where individual "free speech" ends and communal interest in "fair play" begins remains unanswered.

We can begin to disaggregate political authority in Washington. We can move programs back to state and local governments along with the funding to implement them. We can break up gerrymandered districts by substituting an apolitical metric. We can dispense with the dysfunctional tactics of Congress such as cloture and political holds on nominees. These institutions may well benefit individual Senators, but they do not benefit the democracy that sent them to Washington.

There is much to be done to strengthen the electorate, but few seem to have the time or inclination to do it.

## NATURAL RIGHTS

Social contract is premised on a second principle: natural rights. In return for surrendering authority to their elected leaders, government guarantees that certain "inalienable rights" will not be violated. "I demand my constitutional rights" is more than a Hollywood refrain: it is every American citizen's shield against the state's overwhelming power to deny these basic legal protections.

The idea of freedom is central to the democratic tradition. Historically, freedom applied only to the limits on physical confinement.

Over time, the idea has grown into a general concern for the individual and that person's right to life, liberty, and material well-being.

As a political doctrine, natural rights traces its origins to English institutions such as the *Magna Carta* and eighteenth-century philosophers including John Locke and Jean-Jacques Rousseau. The Declaration of Independence enshrined "life, liberty, and the pursuit of happiness." The Bill of Rights added freedom of the press, speech, and religion; the right to keep and bear arms; and the rights to assembly, to counsel, to protection from unreasonable search and seizure, to the presumption of innocence until proven guilty, and to a jury trial.

The Civil War amendments further expanded these rights. The Fourteenth Amendment guaranteeing "due process" and "equal protection of the law" bound the states as well as the national government to constitutional guarantees. Through liberal construction of the "due process" and "equal protection" clauses, the courts have greatly expanded the number of "fundamental rights" to invalidate statutory distinctions based on race, national origin, and sex. The courts have also widened the definitions of "life, liberty, and property" to include public education, public employment, welfare benefits—and privacy. Expansion of the meaning of "life" and "liberty" also underlies the greater procedural protection granted to criminal defendants.

## NATURAL RIGHTS IN HISTORY

Natural rights were enshrined in the first ten amendments as well as in the original Constitution. Several states, among them Massachusetts, Virginia, and New York, included a recommendation with their ratification notes that the new republic pass amendments guaranteeing basic rights. As a principle, the existence of "certain inalienable rights" was never seriously questioned, and omitting a Bill of Rights from the original Constitution proved a major miscalculation on the part of the Framers.

"Natural rights" have been eclipsed by "new rights" that the Supreme Court has discovered in the Constitutional text itself. Most of these new rights, however, are nowhere to be found in the Constitution or documents surrounding it. Examples include the rights to privacy and to certain entitlements. Per se, the Constitution is a living document, so finding new rights is fine. But these new rights then provide the basis for other new rights, such as the right to abortion and the right to make unlimited campaign contributions. Both are even further removed from the original document.

Campaign finance, at least, has some basis in the First Amendment, assuming one concedes that the First Amendment protects more than explicit speech. The "First Amendment freedoms need breathing space to survive," says the Court in *Citizens United v Federal Election Commission* (2010). The larger issue, though, is who defines that space—Congress or the courts.

Whether these "new" rights are or have ever been lurking in the constitutional penumbra is beside the point. Ultimately, these are political decisions that a reluctant but empowered legislature should undertake. Relying on judges responsible for adjudicating opposing legal arguments has forced the courts into far-reaching policy decisions and the undertaking of broad social reform, which they are structurally ill-equipped to handle. At the same time, the legislature has been able to avoid decisions that are properly its own. Moreover, the Framers never intended five-to-four Supreme Court decisions on fundamental policy issues to be dispositive of the republic's core principles. Whether one agrees with the opponents or the proponents of abortion, gay rights, school prayer, and gun control, these are political, not legal issues. To say that the Bill of Rights makes them legal issues is to ignore the practical questions which should be debated in a political forum. Take "gun control" for example. The real question the country should be asking is not whether individuals can have guns, but, rather, how do we prevent situations like Columbine, Virginia Tech and Ft. Hood from occurring?

The Court's pronouncements have extended to blatantly political areas including the 2000 Bush-Gore presidential election and campaign finance. In any legal conflict, each side has the right to present its arguments to the court through counsel. In a political debate, each side should have the right to make its case to the nation through its elected representatives. The media, the courts, and paid consultants are all participants in that process, but Congress and the state legislatures should have the last word. Whether one side prevails or a compromise is reached, the decision should properly belong to our elected representatives, not to judicial appointees.

## FEDERALISM

Federalism is one of the republic's core structural principles. It recognizes that effective self-government rests on a partnership between the national government and one that is closer to home. Restructuring the central authority from a simple unicameral Congress into a complex, self-balancing, three-branched government operating at two levels was one of the Framers' major achievements.

The states' importance in 1787 obscured what the delegates really had in mind: allocating political authority to that level of government best suited to take on specific responsibilities and whose independence served as yet another check on the abuse of power. It also permitted the constituent units of government to be laboratories for social experimentation, leaving room for greater diversity in government. The successful transformation of a largely agrarian and rural society into an industrial society with a population centered in metropolitan areas, and its evolution from a collection of local communities to a unified national society—set in a global context—reflects the wisdom of its authors' original vision.

In the early days, the principle of federalism required adding strength to the national government. The Hamiltonians argued for more national authority, the Jeffersonians for less. But their actions made clear that the national government was here to stay. The Louisiana Purchase and the Embargo Act of 1807 were the acts of Jeffersonian republicans. When the charter of the Bank of the United States was not renewed, James Madison sorely missed the bank when he needed it to fund the War of 1812.

Following the Civil War and well into the twentieth century, Teddy Roosevelt's *Square Deal*, Woodrow Wilson's *New Freedom*, Franklin Roosevelt's *New Deal*, and Lyndon Johnson's *Great Society* accelerated the trend toward centralization.

## Sovereignty

The difference between the two kinds of government—one general, the other local—lay in the tasks assigned to each. The delegates created a federal republic that shared the characteristics of both a confederation and a unitary government. By dividing authority into so many pieces and levels, they destroyed any lingering possibility of "supreme authority." The delegates constructed a practical solution on a spare theoretical base.

Although the word "sovereignty" does not appear in the Constitution, those who talk about the contours of federalism have frequently confronted concepts of "state sovereignty" or "states rights." The Framers addressed the issue of accommodating two levels of government through the sixteenth-century concept of sovereignty.

Back then, sovereignty meant the absolute power to make laws without the consent of the governed.

The Convention delegates agreed that the people had ultimate authority. Most realized that the legitimacy of a democratic regime lodged not in government but in the people's support for that government. Regarding the people as sovereign, however, meant denying sovereignty to both the state and federal governments. In 1787, however, the states were not only very real but the only political game in town.

The delegates never fully resolved whether the federal union resulted from the states' surrendering part of their authority or from the will of the people who split political legitimacy between local and national governments. Submitting the Constitution to state ratifying conventions rather than state legislatures suggested that the people were in charge; mandating that nine states ratify the Constitution before it became effective meant the states had the final word. The states formed the basis for electing the Senate; the population itself determined representation in the House of Representatives. Both approaches work, but political structures that rested on doctrines of separation of powers and federalism were incompatible with any concept of "supreme, absolute, and uncontrollable power."

To an extent greater than they realized at the time, the Framers created a government whose aims and structures corresponded to the conditions of equality and dispersed centers of authority that characterized an agrarian and largely homogeneous society. Its political landscape was dominated by merchant-statesmen and prosperous professionals whose views were shaped by their desire to exploit the country's abundance and opportunity. The new republic required a thoughtful central government to counterbalance the states' more parochial interests to achieve that end.

Federalism was one of the Framers' central innovations. It defines the fundamental relations between a national government that takes care of national issues and local governments that take care of local needs, with both dealing with shared problems. The relations between national and local governments provoked one of the fiercest debates at the Philadelphia convention: calling into existence a government with sufficient popular backing and national powers to effectively govern the nation clashed with the autonomous position in which the thirteen colonies found themselves. Today America remains one of the few nations that takes a bottom-up rather than a top-down approach to defining the powers of the central government.

In the definitive statement of his pluralistic model in *Federalist No. 10*, Madison wrote that "the *causes* of faction cannot be removed, and that relief is only to be sought in the means of controlling its *effects*—and that the means to accomplish this is in the greater security afforded by a greater variety of parties, against the event of any one party being able to outnumber and oppress the rest."[9] That is, in a large and extended republic, one faction will cancel out the other, thus promoting the common good. Moreover, wrote Madison, "the influence of factious leaders may kindle a flame within their particular States, but will be unable to spread a general conflagration through the other States."[10]

James Madison's theory of an extended republic proved expedient at the time of the Constitution. Although Madison's ideas offered a valid redoubt for the state ratifying conventions, they never had a chance to work. Out of Madison's theory of a common good arising from the clashing of multiple interests and factions came not a principled end but a collection of individual interests. The result has been a government that cannot resolve substantive issues at the expense of solving less important ones; and one that allows parochial interests to prevail because the larger community lacks the energy to decide.

Clearly, some good has come out of the clashing of interests between multiple parties. But early on its flaws became apparent. When Congress could not decide on Hamilton's plan to fund the national debt or where to locate the new capitol, Hamilton, Jefferson, and Madison met and worked out the Compromise of 1790. Though the two ends were entirely unrelated, their agreement placed the national capital in the South and backed funding the national debt. Congressional decision making has rarely looked back. Madison's theory of competing factions provided the theoretical basis for the constitutional decision-making process. And his ideas became an early casualty of its implementation.

As the country grew and the interests multiplied, principled compromise became even harder to achieve. Rather than checking and balancing each other, elected officials simply loaded up the wagon with enough benefits to garner a majority vote. The 2010 vote on health insurance reform is a good example: a 2,400-page bill that provides something for just about everyone yet leaves a major issue—controlling costs—untouched. Though the common good may not have been served, interested parties walk away with what they want. In a country with unlimited resources and growing wealth, that's not a problem. When those resources are gone and economic wealth is increasingly concentrated, this approach becomes less viable.

An agrarian and dispersed federalism adjusted poorly to an increasingly industrial and urban society. As the United States continued to grow—and to become more populous and diverse—the authority of the federal government grew as well. The population's greater diversity, the rise of special interest groups, the enormous power concentrated in Washington, and an increasingly global political and economic landscape all worked to diminish the states' role. In itself, that changing relationship was not a bad trend. But as the federal government expanded, it sought to oversee more and more of the responsibilities initially delegated to state governments.

Beyond the failure of Madison's clashing-of-interests model—or perhaps because of it—we now have a national government whose authority has become pervasive. It piles more and more onto its plate and has grown so big that meaningful opposition is difficult. The inevitable result has been a breakdown in one of the fundamental building blocks of our constitutional structure: the distribution of authority to that level of government best suited to exercise it.

This concentration of authority certainly reflects the need for direction in a global world. It also reflects the national scope of many issues and the attention paid to the quarterback—the President. Unfortunately, it has largely erased the lines between what the national government must do and what the states should do.

The states are hardly perfect, and, in many instances, they have written their own epitaphs. One need only look at dysfunctional state governments to understand why. But there are many successful state governments that are smaller. The problem states should be cleaned up, but not used as an excuse to justify a system whose operation has drifted far from its design.

By the 1960s, state governments had been effectively reduced to vassals of the federal government. "The New Federalism" of the 1980s and several Supreme Court decisions in the late 1990s tried to resuscitate the principle, but to no avail.

Can any theory can replace Madison's dynamic model? Certainly he was correct in foreseeing the difficulty in managing a large and diverse country. But instead of predicating a federal model on a system that incorporates an illusory, self-equilibrating compromise, do we need a different federal model that distributes these larger decisions to smaller units of government that can agree or disagree depending upon their individual priorities?

Whether the country should continue down the path of increasing centralization is a contentious debate. The federal government has tried to do it all when it simply can't. And when it does, the one size that fits all is riddled with exceptions and omissions.

In the United States, local governments weren't imposed by a king or dictator; on the contrary, local governments gave up their authority to create a national government. The states' role today reflects a natural evolution of the power of the national government, but their diminished status was turbocharged by events of the past seventy-five years. That pressure ultimately reduced recalcitrant states from equal partners in government to super lobbyists—and not particularly good ones at that. In fact though not in theory, the states have been largely reduced to pleading for funding and special projects rather than fulfilling the responsibilities the Framers designed for them.

What is the answer? Ultimately, it involves disaggregating the power that has built up in Washington. It can be done through a Congress that sticks to national issues such as foreign affairs, fiscal and monetary policy, and immigration. And it can be done by funding state governments to oversee responsibilities that they manage best. For starters, those include education, criminal justice, and health care. A combined approach in which both levels participate embraces the environment, energy, and transportation infrastructure.

Another aspect of federalism relates to the Constitution's mandate in Article IV, Section 4, that "the United States shall guarantee to every State in this Union a Republican Form of Government." Is any state government that cannot balance its budget, depletes its funding for education, and exists in a vacuum of legislative gridlock truly a "republican form of government"?

Finally, what should be the proper balance when local positions on issues like racial prejudice bump up against rights guaranteed in the Constitution? After the Second World War, "states' rights" proved a poor redoubt for justifying segregation. Segregation reflected a policy of permitted state action and allowed local governments to choose how to structure race relations. But it was Congress' unwillingness to intervene that allowed segregation to continue; and it was the Supreme Court's decision in 1896 that gave segregation its legal ballast. Ending racial discrimination reflected the courage and persistence of many individuals—but it was finally catalyzed by federal intervention to enforce Constitutionally-guaranteed rights.

## RESTRAINTS ON A SINGLE SOURCE OF AUTHORITY

"Consent of the governed" implied that the state's single source of authority flowed from the people. Restraints on a single source of authority became the principle by which this authority was divided among government institutions. It operated through a system of checks and balances. First, the delegates created a series of partitions within the government, which also established the government's internal structures: separation of powers, commingled powers, and enumerated powers. Within the legislature, the basis for representation in the Senate and the House of Representatives became the great debate. Dividing government functions among three distinct but interlocking branches provided the horizontal checks and balances the delegates envisioned. Another major innovation, this was the product of untested political theory and pragmatic concerns for the abuse of power. The Constitution also implicitly combines separation of powers with an equally important concept—balance. Each branch had its separate powers, but these powers were designed to complement one another. The delegates' hope was that out of the clashing of interests a principled compromise would emerge.

*Enumerated powers* define the national government's authority and establish the parameters for separation of powers. The Convention debated the authority of the different branches and levels of government at length. What emerged was generally a compromise between those who favored granting the federal government extensive powers and those who sought to limit them.

The delegates went on to engineer restraints outside of the formal government machinery. These included indirect election of the President and the Senate and denying certain social and economic groups automatic representation in the government. The Framers created a durable yet delicate mechanism whose operation relied on institutional balance and capable officials.

Mechanisms whose primary purpose lay elsewhere doubled as governors on the constitutional drive. Federalism served the practical role of organizing and managing a growing republic, while acting as a vertical counterweight to the national government's abuse of authority. Judicial review both separated the judicial function from the legislative and executive and interposed the judiciary between the Constitution, the people, and the legislature. Finally, successive levels of representative government served to implement the social contract and to qualify those occupying national office through a process that emphasized integrity, experience, and ability.

The result has been a dynamic political system, ever searching for equilibrium. All democratically elected governments have faced the same challenge: how to create a responsible government that serves the community and protects the minority while deterring individuals from usurping authority through government office.

## RESTRAINTS ON A SINGLE SOURCE
## OF AUTHORITY IN HISTORY

These restraints, however, have foundered for reasons similar to those undermining federalism. The original checks and balances inherent in restraints on a single source of authority have been transformed from a diversity of contiguous interests into fiefdoms of separate interests, each striving for supremacy and control rather than compromise and consensus.

Restraints on the source of authority flowing from the electorate have been replaced by an expansion of authority both at and among the three branches in Washington. The executive office (of the President), the congressional leadership, and a Supreme Court majority have arrogated decision-making power at the expense of broader participation in the process. That may well be the price we pay as a maturing democracy in a world that demands quick answers, but it has unfortunate consequences for the way we govern ourselves.

The record of the Bush administration is illustrative. The Executive Office led the country into two costly wars, oversaw an economic meltdown, and contributed to an environment of domestic fear and international disdain. Managed by a compliant leadership, Congress did little about it but go along. That is not to say Congress is powerless—it isn't. But rather than serving as a counterbalance, Congress passed when it should have stood up and remained silent when it should have been vocal. Finally, in *Bush v. Gore*, 531 U.S. 98 (2000), the justices of a quasi-legislative Supreme Court share the blame for the costly political and economic fallout from a war that could never be won. (That is not to say that the Obama Administration has performed much better.)

Certainly the relationships among the branches and levels of government should evolve over time. The men who wrote the

Constitution certainly hoped so. But they also believed that the direction was one of principled accommodation rather than polarized confrontation. Instead, the principle of "restraints on political authority" has been replaced by unrestrained grabs for political authority. The spoils are then baked into a fruitcake of ideas that become our regulations, laws, and judicial standards.

The Constitution creates institutions to manage the conflicts between principles and their internal contradictions and levels of importance. Where does liberty end and equality begin? Where does the national government's reach end and the states' responsibility begin? What are the limits of free markets and when can the government intervene? Within the government, how far does presidential power extend and when should Congress assert its authority? When can the Supreme Court exercise its power of judicial review and when does this power trespass on Congressional authority? How much authority is too much, and how much is not enough? These are all questions that deserve our ongoing consideration.

## PUBLIC VIRTUE

The principle of public virtue is implicit in the political hierarchy created by the Constitution. The subordination of individual interests to the greater good of the whole forms the essence of this principle as well as one of the American Revolution's ideals. Early American thinkers reasoned that while virtue is necessary to every state in which the people participate in government, it is fundamental to a state founded on the belief in the people's combined wisdom.

In the absence of forced compliance with the state's demands, voluntary self-sacrifice for the communal good enabled the state to remain united and functional. In an extended republic and a diverse society, individuals from the highest officials to ordinary citizens would make the difference, through behavior that extended well beyond self-interest.

Structurally, the Framers resolved their ambivalence between the delegates' belief in "the people's innate goodness" and their fears about "every man for himself" by including the principle of public virtue in the new government. In addition to the system of checks and balances within government, they created an electoral pyramid through which only the "wise and virtuous" would ascend to public office. With this mechanical structure they sought to erect a series of increasingly higher hurdles to guard against incompetence and political corruption without incapacitating the government.

In addition to licensing self-interested behavior on the grounds that somebody else's equally self-interested acts would cancel them out, the Framers also hoped to create a republic in which an informed citizenry would elect wise and public-spirited individuals to office. The latter, in turn, would use their position to promote the general welfare and to protect individual liberties. The Framers sought to encourage a "natural aristocracy" by providing elected officials with the required experience to run the country's affairs.

Their model provided successive stages of government responsibility to test those who would eventually run the federal government. The Framers optimistically believed that the "base men" at the bottom would somehow become transformed as they moved upward through the political structure. Most members of the revolutionary generation thought that public virtue—defined as a concern for and willingness to subordinate individual and local interests to the common welfare—was necessary to the functioning of any republican political society. They never explained how selfish individuals would somehow be more virtuous than "men of indigence, ignorance, and baseness"[12] as they climbed the political ladder. While frequently referring to an individual's inherent selfishness, they provided no proof of why anyone should act more altruistically when elected to national office.

## PUBLIC VIRTUE IN HISTORY

Public virtue, "the voluntary self-sacrifice for the community's good," is perhaps the most quixotic of the original principles. Looking among themselves, the country's early leaders found ample justification for its existence. The country has not since seen a group of individuals more competent than those who wrote the Constitution and served in the country's early governments. Since that time, the surge of money in politics, rise of parochial agendas within government ranks, the media's preference for sound bites over substance, and the country's divergent interests have contributed to the demise of public virtue. The electoral sieve intended to elevate experienced individuals with reasoned views to high office has been replaced by money and name recognition as the key ingredients for political success. Although successful candidates are generally well-intentioned, they frequently lack the perspective, empathy, and human contacts necessary to govern.

Today, public virtue lies buried under the detritus of nonstop elections, unrestrained campaign finance, and an electorate that simply views public virtue as a devalued trait of elected leadership. It is another victim of a political system that has simply grown beyond its ability to make responsible decisions.

The country's politicians acknowledge the problem but say they are powerless to do anything about it. Public virtue remains an ideal in a system that does not nourish its existence.

## LEGAL PRINCIPLES

Although the Constitution addresses other issues, it remains a legal document. The Framers incorporated four legal principles into their constitutional model: common law, judicial review, the adversary system of criminal justice, and private ordering. The Convention largely focused on the composition and scope of the federal judiciary. The contours of the republic's legal order and its relation to other values would await the enactment of the Judiciary Act of 1789 and Supreme Court rulings for further clarification.

## COMMON LAW

The application of law to societal problems through principled decision making forms the basis of Western civilization and is fundamental to the American republic. Dating from Anglo-Saxon times, the principle of common law developed into the foundation of individual rights that the colonists brought with them from England and incorporated in the Constitution.

"Common law" refers to the general system of law that was originated, developed, and formulated in England and that prevailed in most of her former colonies. Common law can be distinguished from civil or Roman law, which is based on a code; from ecclesiastical law, which is separately administered by the Church; from statutory law, which arises from the specific acts of the legislature; and from command law, with the courts simply an extension of the dominant political party. One of common law's strengths is its ability to grow organically to meet society's changing needs for adjudication.

By including the principle of common law, the Framers built in basic common law features such as trial by jury, which is guaranteed in all criminal prosecutions (and under the Seventh Amendment in most civil cases). The Bill of Rights guaranteed other protections unique to the common law: among them, insulation against self-incrimination, grand jury indictment for serious offenses, and the right to cross-examine witnesses.

Prior to the twentieth century, common law was primarily concerned with deciding the specific rights and liabilities of actual parties before the court. The litigants were those who had sustained an injury or asserted rights in personal property that had been taken away from them. The courts decided questions of law and fact only as to the dispute and parties before them and were bound by prior case law precedent. That has changed with the advent of class action lawsuits involving political, economic and social issues such as smoking, securities fraud, and consumer complaints.

## COMMON LAW IN HISTORY

The principle of common law remains intact. It is the ever-changing core of our legal system that adapts to changes in society. It reflects the decisions of thousands of courts around the country rather than the edicts of a few judges.

Brandon Denning rightfully asks the question, "How much is decided by the common law anymore? At both the federal and state levels, aren't we in an 'Age of Statutes'?"[13] The answer is "yes," but common law provides the foundation on which those statutes are enacted.

## JUDICIAL REVIEW

Borrowing language from the *Magna Carta*, the Framers made the Constitution "the Supreme Law of the Land." By elevating the Constitution over the ordinary acts of the legislature, they departed from the English tradition wherein Parliament had the final say over the country's affairs. An independent judiciary is a key component of the Framers' plan. They explicitly removed the federal courts from the legislative process, but used the principle of judicial review to ensure that the laws passed by both the federal and state legislatures conformed to constitutional standards. That was different from the courts' imposing their own beliefs about what those standards should be. Of course, the question of who elaborates those standards—the political or the judicial branches—is controversial. In Article I, the delegates drew a bright line beneath the constitutional branch responsible for making fundamental policy decisions—Congress; in Article III, they drew another line beneath that branch responsible for deciding "case or controversy"—the Courts.

Though the courts are furthest removed from the check of the polling booth, they are frequently closest to the citizenry when seeking to preserve the republic's most fundamental values. As the last remaining guardians of the social contract, the courts frequently serve as the final refuge of citizens who feel they have been treated unfairly.

Addressing that point, Anthony Lewis observed that "judicial intervention on fundamental issues is most clearly justified when there is no other remedy for a situation that threatens the national fabric—when the path of political change is blocked."[14] Another legal scholar, John Hart Ely, sees "judicial imposition of constitutional values as a last resort—when one or another branch fails to give effect to the aspirations of the peoples of the United States."[15]

Mechanically, the courts also function as one of the national government's three branches in the Framers' dynamic political system. This role has frequently forced the courts to deal with the legislature's failure to serve as the primary arena for making policy decisions.

# JUDICIAL REVIEW IN HISTORY

Judicial review was written into the Constitution and firmly established by Chief Justice John Marshall. Marshall led the Supreme Court to rule decisively on its right to review congressional legislation and executive action. He also cemented the Constitution's ultimate supremacy over relevant state activities as well as the authority of the different branches, and he firmly set the Constitution on a course of judicial elaboration. But did the Framers intend the Constitution to function solely as a legal document? The answer is unclear, but the breadth of its contents suggests it was meant to frame broader political, social, and economic values as well. As a guide to the Framers' larger vision of American society, the structure Marshall advocated provided a narrow foundation on which to judge the many needs of a diverse and growing nation.

Supreme Court decisions in the 1800s—cases such as *Dred Scott* (1857) and *Plessy vs. Ferguson* (1896)—ran contrary to the Constitution's primary objective of balancing liberty and equality. In the 1900s, Theodore Roosevelt's antitrust activities and Franklin Roosevelt's social agenda also encountered a Supreme Court whose views were inconsistent with the country's changing economic and social values. The second half of the twentieth century included decisions such as *Brown vs. Board of Education* and *Roe v. Wade*, in which the Court stepped in to make policy decisions that Congress could not. Whether these decisions would have been better framed to encourage the executive and legislative branches to decide matters remains an open question.

That said, fashioning remedial law shouldn't be confused with making substantive decisions. In many of the controversial court decisions in the 1960s (busing, for example), the courts simply fashioned a remedy to implement the civil rights laws passed by Congress.

Are the judiciary's excursions into nonjusticiable areas really an instance of the courts performing their historic function of "doing what they have to do" where political will has failed? Or do these decisions represent impermissible journeys into fundamental policy decisions that properly belong to the electorate? Clearly, the legislative branch has failed to tackle many important problems, but Congressional failure by itself does not explain "judicial activism." The courts could simply force Congress to take the necessary steps by refusing to adjudicate. Is society better served, then, by accepting the court's piecemeal approach to social policy or by demanding that the legislature take necessary decisions?

Should the republic leave important policy decisions to nine individuals—however learned they may be—who are not popularly elected and who are prone to ideological leanings and confirmed for life in their positions? And how can society set parameters on judicial activity consistent with its proper function: to determine the facts in the case before them, to apply relevant legal principles, and to resolve controversy by applying those principles in a manner consistent with prior decisions and the ends of justice?

Life spans have increased dramatically since the country was founded. Putting a term limit to the appointment of judges and mandating a retirement age would not harm judicial independence. These limits could create a more dynamic and engaged court. Declining to adjudicate certain cases would also force debate of—and agreed solutions to—what are fundamentally political issues. In practice, rather than curbing the justices' independence, a limited term would likely allow the justices to become highly recruited members of the legal community. It's hard to imagine any law firm reluctant to list "Justice Oliver Wendell Holmes, formerly Associate Justice of the Supreme Court" at the top of its letterhead.

Denning again asks, "isn't there a danger that towards the end of the term, Justices might have one eye too firmly fixed on future employment and might be tempted to decide cases in ways that increase their market value?" Of course, anything is possible, but the current system offers little alternative to a court that has become a *de facto* third house of Congress.

Another option is to introduce a constitutional amendment creating a doctrine of legislative preemption. In one form, it exists in the United Kingdom, whose unwritten constitution accords Parliament the final say on all issues in which the state is involved. Parliament is bound by its own traditions and those of England's long constitutional history. As a representative body, the history and consent of the governed serve as a check on precipitous legislative behavior.

The doctrine is undeveloped yet worth considering in the United States. It could be triggered by decisions in areas that are more properly those of Congress. Its implementation would give the legislature the right to overturn Supreme Court decisions on the grounds that those decisions violate fundamental constitutional principles of nonjusticiability or separation of powers. The delegates to the 1787 Convention very much wanted judicial review; what they didn't want was courts making important policy decisions by one vote.

A doctrine of legislative preemption creates a potential problem when the Court curbs congressional or executive branch power – especially if Congress is politicized or reluctant to resolve political disputes as suggested above. American was
founded as an "Article I" democracy, i.e., Congress has the right and responsibility to provide a forum to resolve fundamentally political issues. The Supreme Court structurally lacks the ability to make policy. The answer may lie in a Constitutional amendment that clearly spells out permissible areas of Supreme Court activity and when the national legislature may intervene.

## ADVERSARY SYSTEM OF CRIMINAL JUSTICE

The third legal principle, an adversary system of criminal justice, was predicated on the "every man for himself" philosophy, which held that the "truth" would emerge from the clashing of individuals pursuing their own interests. This model implies that justice is best served when two opposing sides argue their strongest case in front of an impartial decision maker by presenting the pertinent facts and points of law most favorable to each position. It assumed that the objective of truth and justice necessarily coincides with the pursuit of self-interest.

Every legal system has lawyers, but the Sixth Amendment made the defendant's right to counsel fundamental to the constitutional system. As the Supreme Court noted in 1932, "the right to be heard, would be, in many cases, of little avail if it did not comprehend the right to be heard by counsel."[16]

The delegates felt comfortable with the "case or controversy" language reflected in Article III of the Constitution. A court may not hear a legal claim unless it arises from a genuine dispute. A complaint requires a plaintiff with a personal stake in the outcome sufficient to ensure an adversarial presentation of the case. Hence a plaintiff must demonstrate suffering of an actual or threatened injury caused by the defendant's conduct. The "case or controversy" language evidenced the Convention's desire to continue a legal system in which the parties argued their cases before a neutral court that would then render a decision by applying prior case law precedent to the facts presented to them.

## ADVERSARY SYSTEM OF CRIMINAL JUSTICE IN HISTORY

An adversary system of criminal justice is fundamental to America's legal system and is consistent with the clashing-of-interests theories that underlie much of American democracy. That is, the adversary principle suggests that out of the clashing of viewpoints before an impartial judge, justice will be served. Relying solely on adversary justice, however, has detracted from the much larger issue of dealing with the causes of criminal behavior. The courts have narrowly focused on procedural safeguards to ensure that criminal defendants get a fair trial, while the ultimate objective of preventing criminal conduct has been largely ignored. Police, lawyers, and judges, the adversary systems' protagonists, appear only in the final stages of a sad story that begins years before in a broken home, a failed educational system, or communal neglect.

Prosecutors exist mostly to define and present the charges, while defense attorneys seek to keep their clients out of jail or to minimize their sentences. The record of court-appointed advocates suffers from inadequate resources and case overload. Moreover, the means at the court's disposal are generally inadequate to the task: the judge has the option of putting the criminal back on the street, where he will break the law again, or sending him to a prison, where he is further brutalized and educated in criminal behavior.

The underlying network supporting an effective criminal justice system has been weakened by the disappearance of strong family, church, and cultural restraints, which deter criminal conduct. They have been replaced by structural changes in society that, to the contrary, foster the growth and spread of antisocial behavior: the transformation of a local and close-knit rural small-town culture into a depersonalized and anonymous urban society; an increasing gap between wealth and poverty; a cult of random violence reinforced by the media; social media that instantly elevates personal behavior to public spectacle; and changing cultural values that place greater emphasis on material accumulation than on humanistic or social achievements.

A more comprehensive approach to criminal justice would recognize that from society's viewpoint, an adversary system frequently forces officials into counterproductive choices. It attempts to deal with a multifaceted issue by controlling only a small and advanced stage of the problem, diverting attention from effecting an overall solution.

The focus should be on the criminal justice system as a whole. That begins with integrating the various components of the legal, economic, and social orders to create institutions that will first deter criminal conduct, then building a system that will apprehend, punish, and rehabilitate those who break the law.

Related issues include overcrowded prisons, mistaken identity cases, and coordinating police and social services. Mandatory sentencing certainly exacts revenge but does little for rehabilitation. The solutions are many, including arbitration, informal hearings, and effective social programs. Certainly the state has the right to remove dangerous individuals from the street. But an effective system of criminal justice requires recognition that multiple forces ultimately lead to an individual's criminal behavior, and that incarceration as a cultural penalty is a poor substitute for understanding and containing unlawful behavior.

## PRIVATE ORDERING

Fifty years ago, two Harvard law professors, Henry M. Hart, Jr., and Albert M. Sacks, wrote "Materials on the Legal Process." Their intent was to highlight "the complex issues arising out of the interaction of state policies, administrative procedures, and private responses."[17] Their material insists on the law's capacity to serve as a focal point for human interactions. Equally, their reasoning suggests that state intervention might not work any better than the private markets they seek to displace.

The principle of private ordering establishes the individual's right to make decisions and have those decisions enforced by the courts subject to the interests of society and the state. One of the Framers' basic tenets was the right of individuals to shape their own destiny. They do so in the larger context of society: the interplay of political and social institutions that seek to balance one individual's interests with another's as well as those that the community has agreed on. This was an original concept that premised the country's progress on individual action rather than on group behavior. The Seventh Amendment, for example, forbids the states "to pass any law impairing the obligation of contracts."

Hart and Sacks made the case for law as the creation and elaboration of social policy. They emphasized the importance of institutional relationships and legitimacy based on principle and democratic openness. They asserted that "private ordering is the primary process of social adjustment," and they emphasized interaction between private and public institutions with authority allocated according to each institution's relative "competence" to handle the matter.[18] In essence, law doesn't have all the specific answers, but it provides a process for finding them.

## PRIVATE ORDERING IN HISTORY

This principle—the individual's right to order his own affairs—remains a basic element of our economic and social orders. But it breaks down in situations in which individual agreements run contrary to societal needs. These societal needs seem particularly aggrieved in the financial sphere, where actions driven by what amounts to no more than simple greed are expected if not rewarded.

In the late 1990s, financial leaders were able to convince the government to remove financial restrictions. The result:  the near-financial meltdown that occurred in 2008, with ramifications that continue to this day. There were many causes, but one of the most egregious lies in generating trillions of dollars in home mortgages lent to unsophisticated homeowners and sold to unsuspecting investors. Politicians, financial leaders, and administrative officials all joined the party until the market imploded in 2007–2008.

American society is beginning to understand that although financial players may not be physically violent, the damage they can cause runs far deeper and is infinitely more expensive to repair than the one-count criminal complaint.

The country has many competent and honest business leaders. A more thoughtful, open, and vocal business community that expresses its own views rather than relying on public relations' teams might win back the public's trust and contribute to a better regulatory environment. The eighteen-century Irish statesman Edmund Burke said that "evil prevails when good men do nothing." The good men and women of the business community seem more afraid of being wrong than of rightfully speaking up.

## ECONOMIC PRINCIPLES

Economic principles frame the economic ends of government. Those ends include the individual's ability to earn a living; basic needs for food, shelter, and clothing; supporting a family; and contributing to the community. They also include establishing and maintaining a basic public infrastructure: for example, handling budgets, taxes, the post office, roads, and a military defense force; promoting jobs; funding schools; and running airports. Though the Framers were foremost involved in a political act, pressure for the Convention largely arose from economic concerns. In March 1786, James Madison wrote to Thomas Jefferson: "[M]ost of our political evils may be traced to our commercial ones, as most of our moral to our political."[19] As Ralph Louis Ketcham notes, year's later Madison wrote that "regulation of commerce in the national interest had been a prime reason for adopting the Constitution in 1787, [and] that this power had not been questioned in the ratifying conventions."[20]

Settling political issues and establishing political arrangements thus took precedence over shaping the economy. Economic concerns were primarily discussed in the context of the power granted to Congress, the delegates' opinions on socioeconomic class, and the broad debate over slavery. Serious consideration of the primary economic issues involving trade, taxes, and the government's role in the economy didn't occur at the Convention until August 1787. Moreover, these debates mostly reflected the fight over the division of political authority and the effort to ensure that one part of the country did not take advantage of another.

One of the first scholars to examine economics at the Convention, Charles Austin Beard, argued that the Constitution was largely the work of economic elites who sought to advance their own class and financial interests.[21] Later research has largely disproved Beard's theories, though economic considerations loomed large at the Convention. As a group, the Framers were not particularly involved in bondholding or speculative operations, and they were drawn as much from agrarian, commercial, and legal interests as from any moneyed elite.

Beard, though, was correct in his argument that the Framers were, of necessity, commercially astute. The economics embedded in the Constitution largely reflected the delegates' personal business experience. If the Constitution's authors thought about economic theory, they did so in the context of Adam Smith's ideas in *The Wealth of Nations*. The Framers admired Adam Smith for more than just his economic precepts, which supported their notion of free trade. His moral philosophy was congruent with their political views of human conduct and the perceived need to restrain man's selfishness through a self-correcting system of checks and balances. Indeed, one historian has argued that the crucial element of Madison's system is representation, which makes a large republic and a modern commercial system possible along the lines suggested by Smith.

Thus an overall economic construct was left for future generations to develop. The men who assembled in Philadelphia developed a plan and theory of government that applied the era's latest political ideas to solving the practical exigencies of the new republic. Any theoretical overtones represented an extension of their political thoughts and objectives. What they couldn't foresee was the expansion of "free trade" to include "free markets," the enormous growth of global capital and industrial markets, and the expansive role that government would play in what would become the world's largest economy.

## DIRECT BUT LIMITED GOVERNMENT INVOLVEMENT IN THE ECONOMY

The debate over the government's proper place in the economy reflected a deep division between the delegates who favored a strong central government and those who didn't. Madison himself noted that the question was not how to regulate commerce among the several states but the "degree of that regulation."²² Aware of sectional rivalries, the delegates erected an economic infrastructure that encouraged business and balanced regional interests.

Interwoven with both the nature of the marketplace and the government's role were the issues of capitalism and democracy. The delegates knew the importance of economic prosperity to the growth of democratic institutions, and they believed that political equality resulted from economic stability.

The economic principles reflect our commitment to letting the government do what it must but then allowing individuals to do the rest. That philosophy provides the bedrock of our economy and is what distinguishes our country from the rest of the world.

Government interjects itself into the country's economy in three general ways: as a referee, as a regulator, and as an active participant. In a free market system, government is in its strongest position when keeping a level playing field between private parties. But the delegates thought it desirable and even necessary that government involve itself in the economy. That involvement, however, was limited to umpiring the free flow of commerce, regulating certain activities, and providing an economic infrastructure.

The delegates outlined certain economic tasks for the government to perform and decided to omit others. They realized that the national government's support was crucial to the health of the young republic's commercial system. Some favored more government involvement than others, but all agreed that the federal government would play a direct if limited role in facilitating interstate commerce, promoting foreign trade, and furthering the nation's economic progress.

## DIRECT BUT LIMITED GOVERNMENT INVOLVEMENT IN THE ECONOMY IN HISTORY

Government's direct but limited involvement in the economy has long been an accepted constitutional principle. The $64,000 question, of course, is "When should the government intervene?" When does "direct but limited" become "unlimited"? Looking at the country's history, no clear answer emerges. From Jefferson's Embargo Acts to Bush's $780 billion TARP program, government's role in the economy has been all over the map.

The Supreme Court has struggled with the question ever since

Chief Justice Marshall's 1819 opinion in *McCulloch v. Maryland*, upholding certain actions of the Second Bank of the United States. Marshall wrote, "let the end be legitimate, let it be within the scope of the constitution, and all means which are appropriate, which are plainly adapted to that end, which are not prohibited, but consist with the letter and spirit of the constitution, are constitutional."[23] The delegates set down specific limits in the Constitution; nevertheless, the federal government chartered a national bank, purchased the Louisiana Territory, and passed the Embargo Acts. Government intervention continued to expand in the second half of the nineteenth century and throughout the twentieth century.

Government programs have moved beyond "limited" to fill every nook and cranny of the country's markets. Society's demand for more and more goods and services may be real. But the government has borrowed more and more money to fund these projects without regard to the eventual costs or the country's long-term objectives. Other than gimmicks such as reduced payroll taxes, moving items from one fiscal year to the next, and imposing mandatory furloughs, governments have been largely resistant to abiding by a plan.

The budget is a social checklist that reflects America's goals and priorities, allocating funds among competing ends. But, we cannot guarantee a good public education for all children because our money is going to fight wars and buy military hardware; we cannot provide health care for the uninsured because we cannot come to grips with ever-escalating costs; we cannot rehabilitate prisoners because we continue to build more prisons instead of creating new programs; we cannot end the housing crisis or increase employment because the government keeps accumulating private debt on the public balance sheet without providing a road map for growing the economy.

We have reached a point where government has simply grown

far beyond any ability to manage itself. That must change. We must prioritize our goals and spend accordingly.

The United States has been able to borrow because the size of our economy and financial markets create a large asset base. Another reason is our commitment to process, such as the importance of contracts and freedom of expression. People in other countries trust us and buy our bonds. The United States also purchases goods and services, which puts money into people's pockets. As a result, the dollar remains strong, and the United States can print and borrow huge sums of money.

America's advantage begins to erode when we make or purchase goods and services that are consumed or put money into other country's pockets. The money flows out and only indirectly flows back into our own economy. The value of the dollar will also be impacted by the fate of the euro and whether China's remembi will continue to appreciate and internationalize. Both outcomes will determine whether these currencies will be used to settle cross-border trade and become reserve currencies, effectively challenging the dollar for preeminence. For all these reasons and more, the purchasing power of the dollar remains precarious.

Erecting trade walls is not an answer either to defending the dollar or creating jobs. For one, the foundation of today's global economies is the ability to produce goods and services at the most efficient cost. Our costs are generally too high to be competitive beyond our borders (except, for example, in construction and perishables). And if we erect trade walls, our trading partners can do the same. Moreover, creating trade barriers ultimately raises costs and limits the choices of America's consumers.

At a broader level, the boundaries of government action lie in the social fabric of society. Too much government weakens fundamental pillars of American society—individual initiative, private ordering, and fair competition. The founders understood that unrestrained competition is not perfect by any standard. Government intervention in the economy can fill in the cracks, correct diseconomies of scale, and referee disputes. But it cannot substitute for individual effort and the rewards of hard work in creating value and building a successful economy. There is no *a fortiori* reason to believe that government mandarins are better than entrepreneurs or good corporate executives at creating value or allocating capital. Nor can we continue to glorify those who grow wealthy by gaming the system. Naming public libraries or university halls after these individuals simply tells the next generation, "All that matters is how much."

Another important element of the government's role in the economy has been encouraging science and technology. The Constitution commits the government to protecting intellectual property such as patents and copyright. Promoting research and development has long been one of the government's most accepted activities. Our faith in the ability of science to solve just about any problem has made America an optimistic and wealthy nation. But just as often, the limits and undesirable side effects of too much technology have signaled a reliance on pushing buttons rather than asking questions. Still, America remains a global epicenter of new ideas and innovation. In a world in which ideas rather than muscle increasingly determine success, that's an important achievement.

Limitations on government activity have distinguished the United States from other countries in the world and arguably made us the world's largest economy and its oldest functioning democracy. We are not Europe, where central governments have repeatedly exhibited their distrust of open markets. We are not Asia, where government mandarins hold sway. America is a country that believes in the success of private enterprise and individual leadership. A government in overdrive simply vitiates the economic and social foundations that support these pillars of our country.

If the government is to have a role in the economy, the country's leaders should articulate what that role should be. A "new vision" entails building needed infrastructure projects, taking a hard look at where jobs originate (small business), and defining an economic vision for the future. Areas such as education, infrastructure, and social services have been deprived of necessary resources as funds are directed to the military, health care, and subsidies for just about everything. No one at the center of the system wants to or can make a choice.

## FREE TRADE (FREE MARKETS)

The Constitution reflects the Framers' simplified notion of free trade, a precursor to the modern "free markets" concept. The men who wrote the Constitution were not doctrinaire free traders. While they supported tariffs to protect local businesses, they believed in competitive markets. The delegates defined "freedom of trade" as the "unrestrained liberty of the subject to hold or dispose of his property as he pleases."[24] Given the varied economic interests represented at the Convention, "free trade" embodied mutual recognition of each individual's right to pursue his own commercial activity with as little outside interference as possible. Rather than granting "By Appointment to His Majesty" concessions, government would oversee a fair and open economy.

"Free trade" is very different from "free markets," whose theoretical foundations extend well beyond the limited economic structure built by the Framers. "Free trade" generally refers to international trade and the absence of tariffs or other trade barriers between nations. "Free markets" encompasses the way markets function and the relationships between them; and, describes the forces that shape market dynamics and organizational behavior in the modern industrial state.

The economic concepts underlying the Constitution were built to sustain a largely agrarian society moving into the early stages of the Industrial Revolution. This landscape preceded the development of international industrial and capital markets. Industrial markets have grown into global exchanges, while capital markets have developed a life of their own separate and apart from primary markets for goods and services. Smith couldn't have predicted the revolution in transportation, telecommunications, and trade that has made the world's economies highly interdependent. In Smith's day, large enterprises were held by families or favored groups of individuals. The large multinational corporation owned by private investors was far in the future. The imperative of time-based competition was then measured in years, not months; an economically flat world was inconceivable.

Free markets governed by private ordering and government regulation have made the United States a prosperous nation. The government built canals and roads, chartered two national banks, and assisted the railroads. It funded the national debt, passed tariffs, and collected taxes. Two centuries later, it has sponsored the space program, underwritten many technological advances, and bailed out banks and car companies. In the process, though, it has increasingly interfered with the fundamentals of a free market.

The principle of free trade that guided the Convention provided the new nation with a common starting line for the many sectional, class, and occupational interests that existed, rather than a multifaceted economic paradigm. Based on existing economic theory, the delegates created structures and relationships that were not intended to be all-inclusive even in their own time. Their paradigm lacked the complexity and sophistication that free market theory requires to pilot a democratic government in today's global economy.

The United States has largely relied on private enterprise to create the $15 trillion economy that dwarfs those of all other nations. That success has not, however, preempted the need for rules and regulations to protect the system and to deter unfair or fraudulent competition. The challenge has been to define the limits while encouraging the entrepreneur and promoting economic progress.

## FREE TRADE (FREE MARKETS) IN HISTORY

The principle of free trade, which has been enlarged by the principle of free markets, was fundamental to the Constitution. The belief that open and competitive markets provide the best economic result has long been a mainstay of America's prosperity.

Over the past two hundred years, the country has evolved from an agricultural to an industrial and labor-intensive economy, and then to a service- and information-driven system. In the 1890s, the United States passed the Sherman Antitrust Law, which has grown into a formidable means to protect open markets. The United States is also a party to the World Trade Organization, which seeks to protect fair competition internationally.

Today's global economy and markets are infinitely more complex than those that surrounded the Framers. Primary and capital markets have grown into distinct entities, their impact on one another never a certainty. At the time of the Constitution, Smith acknowledged labor's and capital's different objectives, but didn't take into account the separation of management and ownership that would arise in the modern corporation or the global securities markets that exist today.

At the time of the Constitution, the producer funded his operations through retained profits and personally arranged loans. Today's multinational corporations are financed through massive and anonymous sales of public debt and equity. The traditional corporate norm is represented by a pyramid with widely dispersed shareholders at the base and a CEO at the top. New corporate norms, introduced by private equity and venture capital, have challenged this concept with the "plus" model—that is, a model that directly aligns interests between owners, managers, and employees on one hand; and lenders and investors on the other.[25]

Lately, small businesses have become an endangered species. They are under pressure from the economy's poor performance and have had a difficult time raising capital. Many small businessmen (and women) do not understand how to write an effective business plan. Our country could readily support and help entrepreneurs to understand the essentials of starting and managing a business. There is no reason, for example, why high schools (and colleges) couldn't offer classes on the essentials of building and managing a business for those who are interested. Less regulation (with oversight) would also facilitate competing in a difficult and challenging environment.

America's free markets have long been a standard for the unlimited economic opportunity that exists in America. That standard should be modernized but maintained.


## SOCIAL PRINCIPLES

Although nominally silent on social issues, the Constitution also offers a social template for the country. Governments are ultimately created to create or to preserve a certain social order. The Constitution rests on values that expressed and fit the social conditions that prevailed in early America. Among the values that political society was expected to promote were individual liberty and equality of opportunity. It operated against a backdrop of general growth and prosperity, with land, opportunity, and freedom within reach for most white and male Americans.

Though the delegates frequently discussed social class and the manner in which different social strata would be represented in government, the Constitution embodies social principles that address a much broader concern with social and cultural forces competing in a diverse and open society. They assume a pluralistic and equalitarian society, in which individuals are free to exchange ideas, join groups and associations, and speak their minds.

The social principles have evolved with American society. The importance of groups and associations has remained fundamental to our society, if never quite fulfilling Madison's theories; and the limits of an equalitarian society have been exposed as the wealthy grow wealthier and the middle classes more overburdened. Separation of church and state remains fundamental to American society, despite efforts to limit its scope.

## PLURALISM

The principle of pluralism is fundamental to a nation that spans a wide range of peoples and interests. Pluralism holds that the state is less an association of individuals than an association of coequal and cooperating groups. These include churches, professional associations, trade unions, employers, and community organizations.

At the Convention, Madison outlined the pluralistic base for the new government. He argued that "only the inclusion within a government of a multitude of interests, sentiments, and sections, each with power to resist the others, would prevent majority tyranny."[26] Madison's theory of "an extended republic" justified the political principle of federalism, and the principle of pluralism formed its societal base. It functioned through the clashing of multiple interests in a world in which decision making was intentionally dispersed. To simply divide the country geographically, Madison argued, was insufficient. "It was politic as well as just that the interests & rights of every class should be duly represented & understood in the public councils."[27] He writes, "Republican weaknesses were not compounded in an enlarged country; rather by counteracting each other, they were diminished and controlled."[28]

The delegates didn't spend a lot of time on social theory in their debates. Their sociological framework was very basic, and their study of group behavior largely reflected Madison's observation that "the three principal classes into which our citizens were divisible were the landed, the commercial, & the manufacturing."[29] There were many who fell outside these economic bounds—chief among them blacks, women, and Native Americans. It was clear, however, that the delegates understood the importance of group dynamics. The theory of "factions and associations" that Madison and his two *Federalist* colleagues advanced to sell the wisdom of the constitutional model implicitly rested on pluralism and formed the cultural foundation of the Convention's political model.

Madison criticized the destabilizing effect of these different factions, but their existence also added a means of social control to the national government's carefully circumscribed political authority. In a state in which authority was widely diffused and that relied heavily on the voluntary cooperation of its members to maintain order, these factions and associations served many important functions of social control and action. Indeed, the republic's political mechanisms are specifically designed to balance if not harmonize internal conflict between competing factions.

Alexis de Tocqueville wrote, "[I]n no country in the world has the principle of association been more successfully used or applied to a greater multitude of objects, than in America. There is no end which the human will despairs of attaining through the combined power of individuals united into a society."[30] The group serves as a conduit of social power. Groups and associations focus individual action on organizational ends.

## PLURALISM IN HISTORY

Pluralism is the social counterpart to the principles of federalism, adversary system of criminal justice, and free markets. It suggests a society founded on multiple groups and associations that form a heterogeneous and competitive whole. These groups include the family, racial and national minorities, and socioeconomic classes. Madison's political theory assumed a pluralistic society, but his ideas never really worked. Why? The number of groups and associations has grown exponentially. Some groups are bigger or wealthier than others or have been here longer. Rather than a common good arising from their competition, the story of pluralism has been a fight for who can shout the loudest or pay the most. The result has been a cacophony rather than a symphony.

Pluralism remained important as Americans advanced into the frontier and more immigrants reached the new country. Prior to 1880, immigration was virtually unrestricted. Increasing waves of immigration gave rise to "nativist" groups, whose exclusionary beliefs ran contrary to this goal. However, America's pluralist culture and its religious tolerance ultimately helped the nation through this period.

From the Civil War until the end of the nineteenth century is often referred to as the "Gilded Age" or the "Age of Industrialism." These were the years in which America's industrial might grew. Individuals became rich through the railroads, oil, and steel. But an even greater number of people who worked to create these empires remained poor. Chinese laborers on the railway, immigrant workers in Eastern factories, poor farmers, and former slaves who suffered under the Jim Crow laws all built wealth without sharing in it.

Since the second half of the twentieth century, the course of our pluralist society has largely been one of increasing economic divide. Women, blacks, and other social groups have seen their position improve, but the country has struggled with keeping the "golden door" open for foreign visitors and immigrants. Increasingly, economic rather than social status has become the flash point in our country's pluralistic society.

## The Family

Charged with preparing individuals to function in society, the family has historically served as the republic's most important agency of socialization. The twenty-first-century family and its role in American society are vastly different from their late-1700s counterparts. The breakdown and shifting nature of the family unit have caused very real problems that cut across all strata of society. While "family values" retain a central place in American society, the gradual erosion of the family's role in enforcing societal values has forced the state to assume many of the tasks that relatives once performed.

## Socioeconomic Classes

The enduring existence of social classes in a state that theoretically did away with European class divisions isn't easy for Americans to acknowledge. Wealth, family background, and ethnic origin, however, still play an equal role with ability and character in determining an individual's opportunities in society. No state, it seems, can prevent the stratification of society. In a state with a free market economy such as America's, these divisions are likely to take place along economic lines. As long as class levels are fluid and opportunities to advance exist, this danger will be minimized.

## Racial and Ethnic Minorities

The delegates were charged with setting up a government for a relatively homogeneous country. Of the estimated five million Americans at the time of the first census, most were white, Protestant, and of English or Northern European origin. If divisions existed, they fell more along sectional boundaries rather than reflecting any great ethnic or racial differences. But homogeneity gave way to diversity in the early 1800s. America has struggled for two hundred years to eradicate and progress beyond slavery and segregation. The issue still festers, but as a whole the country is committed to racial and ethnic acceptance.

## National Character

The Framers' legal remedy for managing the tensions of a pluralistic society required balancing competing interests through partitioning political authority. Pluralism also demanded the fusion of different cultural traits in the concept of national character and nationhood. The elusive concept of a national character serves as a social counterweight to the republic's diversity.

In 1942, with the nation at war, the anthropologist Margaret Mead described her vision of the American character: "The essence of the Puritan character, the character which has reached its most complete development in America, is the mixture of practicality and faith in the power of God—or moral purpose. Trust in God, my boys, and keep your powder dry."[31]

Other scholars have also contributed to defining the national character. Frederic Jackson Turner was one of the first to look at what made Americans tick by isolating the importance of the frontier and the consequences of what he termed its "closing" for the national psyche.[32] Another sociologist, Louis Hartz, argued that the absence of a feudal past has been at the center of the American intellectual tradition.[33] David Potter suggested that abundance has been the key to the American character. For Potter, the quest for material wealth underlies the mobility and status of the American people, the role of the frontier, the growth of democracy, and America's "manifest destiny."[34]

Though the existence of a national character in a population as diverse as that of the United States is questionable, Americans do seem to have certain common traits. Some are conducive to a vibrant and productive society, others symptomatic of a materialistic and violent society.

The emergence of a distinctly American culture has shaped our image at home and abroad. American literature and art are well known, but it's largely American cinema, twentieth-century music (rock 'n' roll), what we eat (fast food), perceived wealth (Wall Street), military might (Vietnam, Afghan, and Iraq wars), and technological and scientific achievement (Silicon Valley and Kennedy Space Center) that have defined the nation abroad. Still other forces, such as shared crises and competitive sports, have bound the nation's people closer together. In America, at least, national character is an evolving concept. We are undeniably different now from the way we were two hundred or one hundred or fifty years ago. Our challenge is to articulate how we have changed and to understand what those changes mean for our country.

## The Nation

Closely identified with the concept of national character is that of nationhood. If the government is a political unit, and the state is a legal entity, then the *nation* represents a social and cultural ideal. A nation can be identified through common interests and history including language, territory, politics, culture, race, and religion.

The growth of an American nation conceived in historical and cultural terms has centered around and largely defined itself by the values and ideals expressed in the Declaration of Independence and the Constitution. Their birthplace, Independence Hall in Philadelphia, is open every day of the year. Save for a few days on which they are not required, tickets are usually gone by 11 A.M. Even today, the American nation represents a symbol for other nations, signifying freedom, opportunity, hope, and respect for different social, ethnic, and national backgrounds.

## The Farm: Rural America

De Tocqueville adopted the Jeffersonian view that rural America formed the agrarian roots of democracy. Perceptions have not changed much in two hundred years. At the heart of our concern for rural America is an abiding Jeffersonian belief in the nobility of farmers and farm life, which is closely tied to the country's willingness to subsidize farmers—small and large alike. Though America has transformed itself into an urban and industrial society, our rural past still plays a mighty role across American politics.

A modern pluralist social theory should explain how a diverse and dispersed country can intelligently advance the interests of its many groups while resolving conflicts between different social and economic strata. One solution seems to lie in finding a common set of principles that a majority will agree on and respect.

America's strength lies as much in its cultural diversity as in its democratic ideals. The flow of recent arrivals constantly replenishes those ideals and introduces new skills. Historically, immigration policy has centered on balancing the forces seeking to preserve cultural traditions against those working toward assimilation. Today our country, at least, has recognized the value of a multicultural society. But the recent influx of illegal immigrants has added a new dimension to the national debate. How do we balance a diverse society with promoting unity and finding common purpose? How do we integrate new arrivals into a society dedicated to preserving fundamental equality among its inhabitants while protecting the rule of law and rights of its citizens? Ultimately, Americans should recognize that we have always been a compassionate and generous nation and our interests are best served by continuing that tradition. Playing the tough guy has never been our strong suit.

An attempt to solve immigration issues in June 2007 came a cropper for multiple reasons. The debate largely failed to distinguish between, on the one hand, the need for secure borders and enforcing existing laws; and on the other, how to treat the sizeable number of immigrants that have been here for years who play a productive role in the economy but lack proper documentation. We are a nation of laws but also a nation of immigrants. How to balance the two is the question.

Another example of reconciling pluralism with coherent goals is politicians' frequent invocation of "the small farmer" to justify government subsidies to big agriculture. The many agricultural bills are enormously expensive. Who really benefits is an open question. America is not alone among nations granting special privileges to farmers. But taking a principled approach to how we dole out subsidies to industries that no longer need them has taken on greater urgency as the Treasury descends ever deeper into the financial hole.

"Equality" balances "liberty" and suggests that "people who are alike should be treated alike." This definition, however, is deceptively simple and does not address the degree to which the Framers intended that people should be made equal and in what respects.

## The Meanings of Equality

It is easy enough to assert that America has remained a society "dedicated to the proposition that all men are created equal," but as the republic has evolved, the definition of "equal" and the determination of who is included in "all men" have proved more elusive. The principle of equality was explicitly and implicitly central to the constitutional model, but the nature and meaning of this equality have changed over the nation's history.

Development of the principle of equality has been twofold: not only have the ways in which people should be treated alike been expanded, but the ranks of those citizens who are entitled to be treated alike have grown.

*Equality Before the Law.* When the delegates spoke of equality, they most likely meant every citizen's right to receive a fair trial. Legal equality has two major strands. "Equal protection" encompasses the substantive aspects; it means that there shall be no governmental classifications of individuals on "an irrational basis" and that the laws themselves shall be equal laws.

Equality, however, deals as much with access and procedure as with substance. Thus the second strand of due process concerns itself with the methods of government action and has evolved around the requirements of a defendant's right to notice and an opportunity to be heard. "Substantive due process" springs from the fundamentals of "ordered liberty" and is more closely related to natural rights than to an equalitarian society. Equality of rights, however, comes close to what Jefferson referred to in the Declaration of Independence. He didn't totally believe that people were endowed with equal attributes or equal abilities, but he did believe in equality of legal rights.

*Political Equality.* Political equality has come to mean more than equal voting rights; it includes the absence of discrimination at the polling booth on the basis of property, gender, or race. Over the past fifty years, the United States has made great strides in ensuring political equality. The Twenty-Third Amendment removed the poll tax. Voter registration drives and the Supreme Court's "one man, one vote" ruling have further strengthened political equality.

*Economic Equality.* Equality of economic opportunity that ensures equal access to jobs and housing is now considered a fundamental right. In turn, equality of opportunity has led to equality of result, guaranteeing certain minimum standards of material comfort for all Americans. The Constitution implicitly accommodates a society where differentiation of wealth and talent exist without characterizing it as a non-equalitarian society. Today, the question is where the bounds of economic equality lie both in terms of individual wealth and of its impact on how our democracy functions.

*Equality of Opportunity.* Equality of opportunity often boils down to economics. When the Constitution was written, an individual's economic opportunity didn't detract from his or her neighbor's chance to make a fortune. However, that idea of unlimited resources is not an accurate reflection of the world in which we now live. Moreover, the equality of opportunity that has become a popular goal in the past thirty-five years would have seemed radical two hundred years ago.

*Equality of Result.* Government's responsibility to look after the people's general welfare and ensure a minimum standard of living goes beyond the question of equal opportunity. If promoting a "floor for a decent life" becomes a desirable societal goal, who sets the standards and by what criteria? Equality of result should be defined in terms of housing, social services, education, and job opportunities rather than just a blanket statement. But first we must define who is eligible for what, and who pays for whatever result is mandated.

*Social Equality.* The Constitution's authors believed that one of the state's principal tasks was the regulation of the "various and interfering interests" in society. These factions had their source in societal divisions based on the "various and unequal distribution of property."[35]

The delegates rejected the class basis of human superiority, but they "meant only to change the origins of social and political preeminence, not to do away with such preeminence altogether."[36] Although they frequently admitted that the average man was sufficiently good and reasonable to be entrusted with freedom, they created a government of law under which selfish behavior would be checked and a natural aristocracy would rise to positions of leadership.

## Slavery

In creating an "equalitarian society," the Framers focused on a limited legal (and to a lesser extent political) equality. Not all citizens were entitled to vote nor did all enjoy the same legal rights. "All men are created equal" did not literally mean *all* men, as "slaves and their descendants" were excluded.

The prevalence of relative equality made it easy to ignore inequality for blacks. The Southern states' adamant belief that slaves were legitimate property stifled the delegates' debate on slavery and was in great part responsible for establishing economic and social inequality in America.

Although the South's leading statesmen—Washington, Jefferson, and Madison among them—individually owned slaves, they as well as other delegates were opposed to slavery throughout the Convention. The Framers were forced to make a principled compromise, and at some juncture they opted for union over abolition. The delegates believed that a majority of Americans saw the evils of slavery and that it would soon be abolished. These men might well have agreed that their lack of success in resolving the issue of slavery was the Convention's most egregious failure—without in any way implying that the Convention itself was a failure.

## EQUALITARIAN SOCIETY IN HISTORY

Equality's meaning has undergone a transformation over the republic's history. Over the past two and a quarter centuries, however, forces in American life have worked to expand the meaning of equality and to promote egalitarianism.

The equality prevailing during the Revolution began to unravel in the early 1800s. An economic gap widened as more immigrants arrived and as early families grew wealthy. The delegates' failure to end slavery led to the Civil War. After Lincoln's election, the gathering storm burst into armed conflict with the secession of South Carolina and surrender of Fort Sumter in April 1861. Four bloody years of violence followed, ending only with General Robert E. Lee's surrender in April 1865.

America's commitment to equalitarian society sparked legislation in the late nineteenth century aimed at promoting equality. These included the Morrill Act, which encouraged agricultural colleges, and the Homestead Act, which opened land up to those who would work it. Workers organized into labor unions. Laws such as the Pendleton Civil Service Act of 1883 effectively ended the spoils system, and the

Sherman Antitrust Act of 1890 sought to tame the abuses of monopolies.

Theodore Roosevelt continued to pursue America's commitment to an equalitarian society. He instituted reform acts including the Hepburn Act of 1906, which regulated predatory practices of the railroads, and the Pure Food and Drug Act of 1906, which instituted a range of public health standards. Roosevelt also initiated a wide range of conservation acts that greatly expanded America's system of national parks, open to all.

Woodrow Wilson's "New Freedom" also followed an equalitarian path. He passed child labor and workers' compensation bills, all reflecting government's ability to act directly on the economy in pursuit of encouraging an equalitarian society. The 1920s saw passage of the anti-immigration laws of 1924 but also the Nineteenth Amendment, giving women the right to vote. And of course the New Deal promoted labor unions, dealt with financial reform, and enacted social security (among many other reforms).[37]

In its 1954 decision, *Brown v. Board of Education,* the Supreme Court stated that "education is a principal instrument in awakening the child to cultural values, in preparing him for later professional training, and in helping him to adjust normally to his environment. In these days, it is doubtful that any child may reasonably be expected to succeed in life if he is denied the opportunity of an education."[38]

Congress and the courts have sought to reinforce equality in American life. The Civil Rights Act of 1957 was aimed at protecting black voting rights. The constitutional rights of defendants were also strengthened with the Miranda case. And *Baker v. Carr* established the "one man, one vote" rule. The Civil Rights Act of 1964 outlawed racial discrimination in schools and in public places across the country. President Lyndon Johnson signed into law many bills for his Great Society, including funding for education, consumer protection, anti-poverty measures, Medicare, and civil rights. And in 2010 the country enacted a health insurance reform bill under President Barack Obama.

Consistent with the Framers' view, American society has never been a society of total "equality." But mobility between socioeconomic groups has generally been high. Margaret Mead wrote, "[T] he American system is really a classification based on a ladder, up which people are expected to move, rather than an orderly stratification or classification of society within the pigeon-holes of which people are born."[39]

Promoting social equality has been accepted as a legitimate role of the state. Discrimination based on race, color, creed, or national origin in public (and some private) places has been outlawed. In the 1960s and 1970s, fair housing and affirmative action programs replaced "blockbusting"; Medicare and Medicaid were passed to help Americans pay for their health care. In the 1980s and 1990s, the government enacted programs to advance home ownership—a program that came back to haunt us in the 2008 financial crisis. Advocates also passed programs such as the Children's Health Insurance Program (CHIP), expanded health care coverage, and established more enlightened criminal treatment programs. Gay rights have become an important issue as well.

Today, an equalitarian society encompasses much more than what it meant to the Framers. The principle applies to a larger and more heterogeneous society. Just as important, equality has taken on economic and social as well as legal and political meanings. An equalitarian society assumes equality of opportunity, and equality of opportunity presupposes a certain minimum equality of result.

Forces in American life have worked to expand the meaning of equality and to promote egalitarianism. A larger percentage of the population has achieved a middle class standard of living, minority groups are more socially mobile, and colleges have placed increased emphasis on recruiting minorities and disadvantaged students. These programs have elevated educated men and women of diverse social and ethnic backgrounds into business and the professions.

While racial discrimination has decreased dramatically, the gap between the haves and have-nots has continued to grow. The reasons are many. The size of global capital markets has disconnected individual wealth from the means of production. Businesses have grown dramatically, while their earnings have been capitalized at high multiples in public markets and trade sales. Extraordinarily well-compensated executives and financial intermediaries benefit from stock options. Computers and the Internet have changed everything: businesses can scale exponentially, with their owners' wealth skyrocketing apace. At the same time, most wage earners have watched their salaries stagnate.

Another reason for the widening disparity is a tax system that assumes wealthy individuals will invest their capital gains, dividends, and interest payments in new businesses. For most, though, this tax-advantaged income just piles up in the securities markets. Money invested in venture funds or start-ups or expansion stage growth expands our economy. Buying Treasury bonds or trading derivatives does not.

Also, there are simply more people from more places (around the world) competing for jobs in a no-growth economy. The opportunities that existed for the country's first two hundred years are largely gone. Doors that were shut in the 2007–2009 collapse will not reopen; manufacturing jobs have moved overseas; and, workers have been replaced by machines.

Government has multiple channels to bridge this gap. One response is to encourage new opportunities in areas such as exploration, education, and technology. But that will be hard without a serious reordering of our priorities. The truth is, we have spent our capital on wars, transfer payments, and subsidies. We have funded this generation at the expense of future generations. We have amassed an astronomical $15 trillion national debt, which makes funding new programs difficult. Small businesses, a major engine of growth, have been starved for capital and handicapped by excessive regulation. Someone must push the Reset button on our national goals. That has simply not happened.

Finally, the most defining element in achieving an equalitarian society is how we educate our young people. America's education system is founded on the principles of pluralism and an equalitarian society. Elite high schools and universities are no longer the exclusive province of the wealthy. But the vast majority of our public schools are failing in their task to transmit the basic intellectual skills of an informed society to a majority of their students.

When groups with better education and better jobs grow distant from those in other social strata, everyone suffers. As one sociologist observed, access to a better education and family surroundings has come to mean that "today's rich don't exploit the poor; they just outcompete them." We are an open society, so we find it difficult to trespass on the prerogatives of our top institutions. But we can spread the national wealth to encompass a larger number of schools that offer superior education.

We should also insist on making our colleges and universities institutions of higher learning rather than feeder schools for the ESPN Nation. Americans love sports. For many, both participation in organized sports and cheering professional teams and athletes are an integral part of how we spend time growing up and how we entertain ourselves as adults. But we should ask whether training athletes for the NBA or NFL is a role that our colleges and universities should play. And if it is, should it be a four-year course? For the vast majority of athletes who do not qualify for professional sports teams (and for many nonathletes), we must ask ourselves what kind of education they have received. Would it not be better to insist that those who matriculate spend some period as full-time students before their professional training begins?

We should admit that not everyone has the skills or interest to attend a four-year undergraduate institution. We should create programs tailored for these individuals so they can become productive citizens rather than pretending to give them an education that few of them will actually receive.

Finally, teaching is a critical vocation, and this country should honor its educators. But, the standards for how teachers are hired, their performance in the classroom, and criteria for granting tenure in K–12 should be examined. In the primary grades, the departure of able women who have taken more lucrative jobs in law and business has been a major loss. The consulting gigs, advisory roles, and entrepreneurial activities of all too many university professors cut into teaching time. We should ask ourselves: what is the purpose and role of higher education? If it is anything less than encouraging our students to obtain knowledge, ask questions, and solve problems, then we as a society have not succeeded at educating the next generation. Moreover, not all students are destined for college. Imparting the basics and then allowing others to learn a trade or skill is equally vital.

Alongside public education, other avenues to connect the haves and have-nots, such as military service, no longer exist. The armed forces, which were a mirror of our society in World War II, have

become increasingly segregated from society at large, both economically and socially. No one ever said that college student draftees
make better soldiers; their serving with their fellow citizens, however, makes a better army and, ultimately, a better society. Our public
schools and the military have become the realm of those who cannot afford better. The results are governing and social elites who are
insensitive to the needs of their societal peers if for no other reason
than that they rarely encounter each other.

The aftermath of the 2007–2009 economic meltdown has further
eroded an equalitarian society. The crisis has raised the prospect of
high, systemic unemployment, while the collapse of the mortgage market has exacerbated the housing woes of many Americans. Credit is no
longer freely available for small businesses, and Wall Street's ways have
worsened Main Street's woes. Who will create the jobs? Is owning a
home an inherent right in America? How should health care be paid
for? What are the limits of low-cost public education? Who pays for essential services—hospitals, roads, police and firefighters? How should
we tax the wealthy, who enjoy most of the tax benefits and also contribute the greater portion of total taxes to government? These are all hard
questions whose place on the national political agenda should be high.
They go to the very heart of what we mean by an equalitarian society.

## SEPARATION OF CHURCH AND STATE

The separation of church and state ranks among the republic's fundamental principles and is firmly stated in the First Amendment. The
Framers were deeply religious men and recognized religion's importance
to an orderly society. Religious liberty stands out as the one subject on
which Madison took an absolute, undeviating position throughout his
life. He argued repeatedly that freedom of religion enhanced both religion's intrinsic vitality and its contribution to the common weal.[40]

In his *Memorial and Remonstrance Against Religious Assessments* (1785), Madison wrote, "torrents of blood have been spilt in the old world by vain attempts of the secular arm to extinguish religious discord by proscribing all difference in religious opinions." He continued, "the preservation of a free government requires that [government] not overleap the great barrier that defends the . . . equal right of every citizen to the free exercise of his Religion according to the dictates of conscience."[41]

The Framers saw the suffering and carnage that protracted religious wars had caused in the past. Justice Hugo Black, in a 1947 majority opinion, wrote, "In efforts to force loyalty to whatever religious group happened to be on top and in league with the government of a particular time and place, men and women had been fined, cast in jail, cruelly tortured and killed."[42] More important, in a democratic society, individual conscience—not state sponsorship—should define religious practice.

Of the many different forces that might destroy the fabric of American society, the Framers were most concerned about those created by religious strife. They hoped to contain political confrontations through an extended republic and internal checks on government power; they relied on an adversary system to settle legal matters; and they believed that competitive markets would determine economic success. For religious conflict, however, a secular remedy didn't exist. Religion and morality were simply not amenable to structural compromise.

When the colonies were founded, not only was the Church a more powerful and established force than the state, but most early settlers never doubted traditional assumptions concerning the state's role in supervising and supporting religious institutions.

Many early communities had sought to duplicate established state churches, but from the beginning there were impediments.

The Revolutionary War hastened the disestablishment of organized religion. The establishment issue remained alive, however, through the eve of the Convention. In 1784, establishment forces in Virginia sought to enact a bill "which would require all persons to pay an annual contribution for the support of the Christian religion or of some Christian church or denomination which the taxpayer might designate."[43] Proponents argued that "since organized religion was beneficial to the general welfare, all citizens should be required to participate in supporting it."[44] The legislators rejected this proposal. Madison's Memorial and Jefferson's Bill for Religious Freedom were passed in its place in 1786.

On the eve of the Convention, the Framers viewed the separation of church and state "not merely as an adjunct to religious freedom, but as an independent prerequisite to a free society."[45] The delegates never discussed the separation of church and state except when the broader Bill of Rights was introduced. The fact that separation of organized religion from government was not an issue shows the extent to which consensus had already been reached by the time the delegates met in Philadelphia. Implicit in the Constitution itself, the First Amendment formally incorporated this principle into the Framers' model.

The First Amendment's establishment of religion clause was enacted, in Jefferson's words, to erect "a wall of separation between church and state." In *Everson v. Board of Education* (1947), Justice Wiley Rutledge's dissent notes, "[T]he Amendment's purpose was not to strike merely at the official establishment of a single sect, crowd or religion, outlawing only a formal reaction such as had prevailed in England and some of the colonies. It was to create a complete and permanent separation of the spheres of religious activity and civil authority by comprehensively forbidding every form of public aid or support for religion."[46]

Though the Constitution only addresses federal establishment,

Massachusetts and Connecticut maintained an "established church" into the nineteenth century: Connecticut's "establishment clause" expired in 1818, Massachusetts' law in 1835.

## SEPARATION OF CHURCH AND STATE IN HISTORY

The Framers were deeply religious men and recognized religion's importance to an orderly society, but they never confused the state's interest in public morality with an individual's right to worship as he or she pleases. They were determined to make an inviolate separation between citizens' personal faith and public politics and laws. Although religious prejudice has existed as long as organized religion, religious intolerance continues to diminish.

### *Modern Interpretation: Separation and Accommodation*

The principle of separation of church and state rests on both legal and social foundations. The Supreme Court, though, has never developed a fixed rule per se, and Congress has avoided the issue.

Deviating from rigid separation, the Supreme Court has consistently recognized that the outcome in establishment clause cases turns on the balance struck between separation and accommodation. The Court has permitted accommodation only in instances in which a secular rationale has diluted the religious meaning or content of the practice in question.

Former Chief Justice Warren Burger's observation that "there is an unbroken history of official acknowledgement by all three branches of government of the role of religion in American life from at least 1789"[47] strikes closer to the divide. The delegates probably did mean to erect a wall between church and state, but they assumed that religious institutions on the other side would retain their central role in society. Noninvolvement didn't translate to indifference.

## Religion's Role in Society

The Framers intended that religious values play an important role in American society. Whether they could have foreseen or imagined society's secularization or religion's decline is doubtful. That the courts have taken the separation doctrine from Madison's absolute prohibition to one of relative prohibition follows the evolution of American society and its greater tolerance for religious differences.

Religion's role has varied from simply infusing a materialistic culture with certain moral and ethical values to providing a focal point for community life. Religious institutions have long provided a meeting place for young and old alike while promoting values and beliefs that transcend those of the workplace.

Religion's influence on national life is both a cause and effect of the importance of moral principles in America. Injecting evangelism, church membership, and other religious issues into the nation's political and economic debate is a basic American theme.

Puritan America was a theocracy, and even though church and state have since been separated, the clergy have been leaders in the social order as well as influential in political and economic events.

Today separation of church and state is an established principle—subject to what the courts believe that separation should be. The Constitution's authors were explicit: religion would play an important part in American life, but the state would play no role in religion. As one observer has noted, the founding fathers believed that religion is best promoted by leaving it alone. That seems like a simple and sensible prescription.

National security is not bound in political, economic, legal or social terms. National security is aimed at guarding the national interest—the state's survival and safety as well as its pursuit of economic growth and societal norms. The Preamble to the Constitution identifies two dimensions to national security: to "insure domestic Tranquility"; that is, to protect Americans from domestic violence; and to "provide for the common defence"—to protect the country, its people, and its values from foreign threats.

In Article I, Congress is granted the authority to provide and maintain an army and navy, to decide when to call out the state's militia, and to "suppress Insurrections and repel Invasions." Section 10 prohibits the states from engaging in war unless there is an imminent threat of invasion. Article II, Section 2 makes the president the Commander in Chief, and gives the executive the power to make treaties and appoint ambassadors. And Article IV mandates that the federal government shall guarantee a republican form of government for every state and protect the states against invasion and domestic violence.

## What Is the National Interest?

What is America's national interest? Domestically, those interests include protecting citizens from crime, domestic violence, insurrection and terrorism. Overseas, those interests include defending America's safety as well as safeguarding the activities of our citizens and businesses. Advancing our national interest also means promoting our core values: political liberty and economic opportunity.

The principle of national security is the basis for government activity that protects our citizens at home and abroad. It requires coordinating national, state, and local action.

## Protection from Domestic Violence

Initially, national security at home translated to protecting the frontier; securing trading rights along the Mississippi; and guarding against rebellion. National security evolved over the course of the nineteenth century. It sought to contain the violence that preceded and continued throughout the Civil War. In the course of the ensuing 150 years, it has meant everything from policing labor disputes to dislodging supremacist groups to guarding America's borders.

Today, national security at home has grown complex. Domestically, many issues demand our attention including safe borders, school safety, protecting our airports and ports, and preventing crime. The response to the September 11, 2001 terrorist attacks represents one extreme—defending against foreign enemies on American soil. National security also encompasses protection against chemical and biological terrorism, the fight against drug cartels, and defense against cyber-terrorism. An even broader definition would extend to issues such as climate change, energy policy, failing schools, and economic dislocation. All erode our safety, security, and national values.

## Protection from Overseas Threats

Following the end of the Revolutionary War in 1783, the country remained ever watchful for attacks on the frontier while steering a neutral course between warring European governments. Through-

73

out most of the 1800s, national defense focused mostly on Europe. By the end of the century, Asia had grown in importance. America fought in two world wars on foreign soil to protect our values. In the years since, America has continued to fight foreign wars of varying relevance to protecting our national interest.

In the early years of the republic, President John Adams had to navigate quarrels among European powers. His successor, President Jefferson, acted to protect American sailing vessels against the Barbary pirates in the Mediterranean, secured the Louisiana territory, and implemented the ill-fated Embargo Acts. Numerous skirmishes with France and Spain forced the national government to use force in insuring domestic tranquility and providing for the common defense. "Manifest Destiny" meant denying Native American and foreign territorial claims in North America. Yet throughout the nineteenth century, U.S. foreign policy was governed by the tenets of neutrality and noninvolvement.

As the twentieth century dawned, the United States could no longer ignore events across the oceans. Our national security required more and more attention to Europe and Asia. The Spanish-American War not only disrupted relations with Spain but tested America's commitment to national self-determination. The Root-Takira Agreement with Japan and the "Open Door" notes of 1899 in China reflected America's growing awareness of Asian geopolitics. World War I thrust the United States openly into European affairs. But the country still stubbornly clung to its long-held position of noninvolvement.

By the end of World War II, the industrial strength of the United States and the destruction of Europe pushed the country onto center stage. There was little time, however, to develop a thoughtful and coherent foreign policy.

Nearly half a million Americans lost their lives in World War II, but the battle against totalitarian government was not over. The war's end was followed by rebellion, revolt, and civil war around the world. Our allies were economically destroyed, Stalin's aggression threatened European stability, and anticolonial movements arose in Africa and Asia. If the United States had had the luxury of time, our policies for the next sixty years might have been different. Was Mao's victory in China a win for communism or a final rebellion against five millennia of dynastic rule? Was Vietnam another domino in the spread of communism or a war against foreign domination? Were African leaders embracing communism or asking for national recognition after centuries of colonial abuse? At home, were we fighting communism or was the United States on the cusp of a major cultural revolution—one that would see blacks, women, and youth upend an established social order?

American politicians never defined events in broader terms. We worried about communist expansionism when far more was at stake. The Iron Curtain fell across Eastern Europe, and civil wars broke out, including those in China, India, and Vietnam. For the first time, the NATO treaty committed the United States to the aid of overseas nations. We came to Europe's defense with the Marshall Plan. The Truman Doctrine aided Greece and Turkey. President Truman was the first to extend *de facto* recognition to the new state of Israel. We backed the South Koreans when they were attacked by the North.

The birth of the atomic bomb added a deadly edge to potential policy failures anywhere on the globe. Nuclear proliferation was added to our long list of national security issues.

At home, post-war economic shortages, the demobilization of the armed forces, and the stirrings of the civil rights movement affected domestic politics. McCarthyism swept the country until finally defeated by its own bombast. Forces that would forever change America erupted in the late 1950s: the civil rights movement had begun in earnest. The baby boomers set a new course that would "shake, rattle, and roll" American society out of its postwar complacency.

President Eisenhower "went to Korea" to end the Korean conflict. He responded to the Suez crisis, the Hungarian revolt, and the Russian space program. Other incidents included the U-2 spy plane incident and Castro's revolt in Cuba. President Kennedy faced the Cuban missile crisis and sent our forces deeper into the mountainous jungles of Vietnam. In Europe, America still confronted a divided Germany. Military juntas took control throughout Latin America. At home, we struggled with the civil rights movement and the Vietnam War. The assassinations of John and Robert Kennedy and Martin Luther King, Jr., were enormously disruptive. Radical political groups such as the Students for a Democratic Society (SDS), the Black Panthers, and the Weathermen all tested the limits of internal national security. President Johnson's policies in Vietnam ended his presidency.

From 1968–2008, seven presidents moved through the White House, and none enjoyed any respite from urgent national security concerns. The United States sent its troops to fight in Vietnam, Somalia, Grenada, Lebanon, Panama, Kuwait, Iraq, and Afghanistan. After communism, we fought terrorism. We sought peace between Israel and its neighbors, watched as the Berlin Wall fell, and helped to mediate between India and Pakistan.

President Nixon negotiated the Strategic Arms Limitation Treaty (SALT) talks, arbitrated the 1973 Arab-Israeli War, and improved relations with China. President Carter presided over the Camp David accords, the Soviet occupation of Afghanistan, and the Iranian Embassy debacle. President Reagan faced Iran-Contra and the attack on the Marines in Lebanon. President George Bush dealt with the Panama invasion, the liberation of Kuwait, and the collapse of the Soviet Union in 1991. President Clinton's national security agenda included

NAFTA, the Haitian intervention, and bringing an end to Serbia's "ethnic cleansing." President George W Bush initially followed a path of unilateralism, then launched wars in Afghanistan and Iraq. Difficulties with Iran and North Korea also surfaced. President Obama inherited the Bush wars in Afghanistan and Iraq as well as the threat of nuclear weapons in North Korea and Iran.

Over time, the country has moved from President Washington's advice to "avoid foreign entanglements" to President Bush's and President Obama's full-scale intervention in countries around the world.

## "American Exceptionalism"

Since its origins, American policy has been colored by a belief in American omniscience. "American Exceptionalism" is not just a phenomenon of the past fifty years; it has reoccurred regularly throughout our history. Ketcham notes, "The great miscalculation of the Jeffersonian administration . . . left a chasm between the principles it proclaimed and the power and means to give them effect."[48] This dogma regularly appears in slogans such as "manifest destiny" and "making the world safe for democracy" and "unique superpower."

Today, our belief that "America is the world's unique superpower" interferes directly with pursuing our national interest. Is our hegemony—unilateral dominance—real? Or does it simply reflect an America-centric view of the world that clouds our view of what is really happening in the world?

In the country's early years, national security meant keeping the peace domestically, responding to foreign threats, and protecting our economic interests. As the nation matured, national security evolved into promoting our ideals around the world. By the end of World War II, America had moved from a confederation of states jealous of its neutrality to a unified nation actively advancing its fundamental beliefs overseas.

At the end of eight years as Commander in Chief, President Eisenhower realized the potential for abuse that a large military created. He warned Americans to "guard against the acquisition of unwarranted influence by the military-industrial complex." He added, "[T]he potential for the disastrous rise of misplaced power exists and will persist. We must never let the weight of this [military-industrial] combination endanger our liberties or democratic processes."[49]

His words have gone largely unheeded. In the fifty years since Eisenhower's remarks, America has marched from one overseas war to another, from covert actions to "regime change," from fighting revolutionaries to combating terrorists. For FY 2012, total requested defense spending stood at $648.7 billion. (Including many military-related expenditures that are outside the Defense Department budget, expenditures stood at well over $1 trillion.) Compare this with China and Russia, the countries ranked next highest on the list of national military expenditures: for 2012, their defense expenditures are estimated at just $91.7 billion and $63.4 billion respectively.[50] And it's unclear what the lives lost and dollars spent on combat missions and military hardware have bought us. Our armies fought valiantly but failed in Vietnam just as the French failed there; in Iraq, just as the British did; and in Afghanistan, just like the Soviets. None of these were wars that could ever be "won" in any accepted sense of the word.

Just how singular is our superpower status? In his 2001 book on foreign policy, former Secretary of State Henry Kissinger wrote, "at the dawn of the new millennium, the United States is enjoying a pre-eminence unrivaled by even the greatest empires of the past. From weaponry to entrepreneurship, from science to technology, from higher education to popular culture, America exercises an unparalleled ascendancy around the globe."[51]

Kissinger's conclusion was his own assumption. It simply

disregards the achievements and needs of others—and our own shortcomings. At the end of World War II, Europe and Asia were destitute, Africa a colonial landscape. With the outbreak of further armed conflicts after the war, American foreign policy should have looked for underlying causes. We didn't. Economically, we built a strong industrial economy, but we let our transportation, energy, and education infrastructures deteriorate. America's movies, music, and language have penetrated the world, but so have aspects of other cultures.

Of course, battles drag on. The Israeli-Palestinian conflict is now over sixty years old. North Korea is as erratic as ever. Iran is bent on developing nuclear weapons. Afghanistan and Iraq remain battlegrounds. And new regimes raise challenges in regions such as the Middle East and South America. But nations rot from within as often as they are conquered from without. If we continue to presume a singular omnipotence that diverts critical resources from protecting our national interest, then we risk losing what has made America unique.

The Soviet threat—like the Soviet Union itself—no longer exists. Did the Soviet Union collapse because of President Reagan's Star Wars program or because the country imploded from its own internal contradictions? China has grown into an increasingly prosperous if centrally ruled country. The Chinese Communist Party's economic theories have evolved without America's help. Sooner or later its politics will as well.

The Vietnam War should have put an end to American overseas military action. How could U.S. armies trained to fight with tanks on broad plains win a war against a foe located thousands of miles away and fighting in mountainous jungles?, We thought we could win, but we couldn't. The reunified country of Vietnam continues to progress, but now on its own course.

Al Qaeda, the globe's leading terrorist organization, has seen its power diminish. Why? The death of Bin Laden helps; in addition, Arab nations are beginning to understand that there are paths to a better society other than a return to an eleventh-century caliphate. Terrorism and guerilla warfare have existed for as long as there has been armed conflict in society. Conflicts can be resolved through force or through equally viable political and social change.

In short, success in maintaining America's national security depends on finding a new central premise for U.S. foreign policy and its domestic counterpart.[52]

Who are we fighting now? What are our objectives? Can we look back to 1945 and ask ourselves, in the best of all worlds, what policies should the United States have followed from that point? How has the world changed over the past sixty years? How can our policies evolve into a solid foundation for a strong country in an interconnected world?

The object of any government, both at home and abroad, is to control the extremes rather than be controlled by them. We have allowed ourselves to be taken in by individuals and groups, in the United States and overseas, whose ends are detrimental to our own but whose means fall far short of threatening our national interest.

We should grow comfortable living in a world in which most people share the same needs and desires that Americans do. The question, of course, is how we deal with those who don't—but modern transportation, global communication, and interlocking economies have brought us all together. It shouldn't be that difficult to live in harmony with other nations who share similar ends but whose means and values differ from our own.

Communism and totalitarianism are dying breeds; terrorism is a lethal but limited force. Yet we have not redefined what our national security entails. In America, unemployment, depleted education programs, national debt, attacks on our digital infrastructure, a deteriorating physical infrastructure, and energy shortfalls should have long since drawn our policy agenda away from other threats. Asian economies have burgeoned, Europe remains comfortable in its social conventions, and Africa demands our attention. The frontiers of science and humanity beckon: we are challenged to explore the bounds of space and the depths of earth's oceans; to look at ourselves and the causes of disease under the microscope; and to preserve an environment that can sustain yet economically support the human race. Those are our challenges, and where we should place our resources and energy.

## PRINCIPLES AND POLITICS

Politics without principles is an empty suit. Policy seeks to formulate politics in the context of specific principles. It defines the means and objectives for legislative and regulatory action. In the United States, debating policy has been far easier than implementing it.

In June 2009, President Barack Obama's administration published a white paper, *Financial Regulatory Reform: A New Foundation.*[53] Whether or not one agrees with its conclusions, the report may well be a first: an effort to outline government policy in a specific area, namely financial regulation, which serves as the basis for political action. The report was written and largely forgotten.

Rarely is legislation the product of asking what we want to accomplish and how we get there; typically it is the result of packaging competing interests into legislation that will garner executive and legislative approval. Maybe that is what American politics is ultimately about. But in a country whose differences of opinion and divergent interests are ever increasing, nonstop legislation is no substitute for a principled vision of what we need to do to get to where we want to be.

Politicians say they can't do anything about the problems in government. And because they can't, they simply go along with them. Moreover, winning elections has become an end in itself. Individuals run for office; they rarely run to advance a broader agenda. We have created a class of career politicians, many of whom continue to run simply to put another notch in their political belts.

Americans are great problem solvers, but we cannot solve problems we don't know exist. The antidote, a free press, all too often reports only what they have been told.

Why doesn't the electorate hold elected officials accountable? In fact, voters do. They generally believe that their representatives are fine—it's "the others" who are scoundrels. And there is the problem of geography. Washington, D.C., and the state capitals lie far from their constituencies. Keeping up with what is happening in the city council is hard enough, let alone following the actions in a state capital that is miles away by road and light years away in political decision making. "The Beltway" is even further removed from the electorate. Nature abhors a vacuum, and lobbyists have rushed to fill the void. The Center for Responsive Politics reports that between 1998 and 2009 the amount that organizations spend on lobbying each year soared from $1.4 billion to $3.5 billion.[54] Between taking care of their contributors and minding their constituents, our representatives have found it difficult to form a principled consensus on any issue.

Finally, the current lack of clear policy reflects what happens to federal and state officials after they are elected. They may be champs on election night. But in capital cities, they are faces in the crowd. We have a two-party system that is organized largely on the basis of seniority. Those at the bottom of the food chain and in the minority have little impact; those at the top and in the majority have a lot to say. Members of "the leadership" control many facets of the political world. They make life easier or more difficult for those at the base of the totem pole; their decisions influence a member's chances for reelection. Where is your office and where do you park your car? How many people are on your staff and who are they? Will the bill you introduced be discussed or forgotten? How do you spend your day, what "fact-finding trips" do you take, and what committees do you sit on? All depend on the junior legislator's relations with the leadership. More important, the leadership decides how much money you get from the state or national party to finance your campaign. It is a rare assembly representative or member of Congress who can or is willing to buck this system.

In short, the quest for policy remains largely unfulfilled. There is no compass, no road map that allows our elected officials to chart a course. In the end, "that's politics" has become a coffee shop one-liner ending the conversation on why things are what they are. But denial is not an answer.

*   *   *   *   *

This essay seeks to define the fundamental objectives of the American republic and to identify the principles vital to their realization. The past sixty years have witnessed a growing distance between the principles as they were conceived and their meaning (if any) today. If the best of what America has accomplished—unprecedented political liberty and unlimited economic opportunity—are worth preserving, then the principles of the American republic are worth revisiting.

Our political decision-making power is not distributed among thirteen colonies but highly concentrated in Washington. That has left the federal government with too much to do and the states with no money to accomplish what they need to do. Our judicial system has assumed a political agenda that it is structurally ill-equipped to handle.

We have an economy that has drifted far from its free market origins. Our government has taken on roles that short-circuit the private sector. The economic equality that largely existed in post-Revolutionary America has been replaced by a hardening divide between the haves and have-nots. While bankers and traders earn multimillion-dollar salaries, many Americans must work two jobs or more to make ends meet. Looking to the future, for perhaps one in five Americans there will be no jobs: structural unemployment and widespread underemployment will persist as Western economies stagnate and corporations continue cost cutting. Those who are securely employed may not understand what all the fuss is about. Those who aren't wonder why their government has spent billions to support an economic system that has done very little for them.

Our society has largely forgotten its pluralist roots—"Out of many, one." For many today, this motto has been replaced by "What's in it for me? And forget the rest." We live in a nation that has heavily mortgaged its future because its citizens cannot agree on the present; one that bullies its way overseas for goals that may be worthy but whose ends can never be achieved.

The government has yet to respond with a larger vision of our competitive strengths and new opportunities. The key to America's future, education, continues to see its funding reduced and programs cut. Infrastructure, housing, and social services are all feeling the impact of an economy ravaged by open-ended entitlement programs, short-term stimulus packages, and never-ending military programs. Despite fourteen million in undocumented immigrants, the country has no immigration policy. A political decision-making system designed for three million living in thirteen contiguous colonies struggles to cope with a diverse nation of 310 million people spread across a continent.

In the end, we have a strong but divided nation. We are immobilized by the present when we should be planning the future. As a country, we are broke financially, though our size has bought us time. As we rethink our place at home and abroad, we should be asking ourselves many questions. We should put aside lesser issues that consume our political energy and talk about fixing our economy, the limits of our military power, the importance of education, and revitalizing our government process. The answers to these questions are much tougher but vital to our survival as a democratic society.

A fix requires a personality change—a rethinking of our fundamental values and what is most important to us as Americans and as citizens of an interdependent world. Without a viable political framework and sound economy, our society cannot spark the collective will to move forward. The ultimate solution requires a socially open, fiscally responsible, and politically principled answer.

Americans will continue to debate the ends and means of our government, economy, and society. But if we don't ask for the government we want, we will get the government we deserve. For better and worse, that is the government we have today. If it is to change, and it will change, there must be individuals willing to articulate and implement what that requires. Like the Marines, America is waiting for good men—and women—to step forward.

# II. Sources of the Principles

The principles' sources lie in the debates, letters, and notes that surround the Constitution. George Washington himself underscored the challenge the Convention delegates faced on June 28, 1787: "We have gone back to ancient history for models of government, and examined the different forms of those Republics which having been formed with the seeds of their dissolution [that] now no longer exists. And we have viewed Modern States all around Europe but find none of their Constitutions suitable to our own circumstances."[55]

The principles may also be said to articulate a theory of the American state; that is, together they describe the conception, means, and ends of our state's decision-making process. Although more of a European concept, a theory of state is worth considering in an American context.

The sources of these principles are more clearly identified in this appendix.

## Social Contract

The principle of social contract can be seen in the repeated references to the role of "the people." On June 6, 1787, James Wilson emphasized that "vigorous authority [is] to flow immediately from the legitimate source of all authority."[56] When looking for a means to approve the Constitution, George Mason stated, "[W]hither then must we resort [to approve the Constitution]? To the people with whom all power remains that has not been given up in the Constitution derived from them. . . . this doctrine should be cherished as the basis of free government."[57] In an extended speech on June 27, Martin noted, "[T] his principle of equality, when applied to individuals, is lost in some degree, when he becomes a member of society, to which it is transferred."[58] Said Madison on August 31, "[T]he people were, in fact, the fountain of all power, and by resorting to them, all difficulties were got over."[59]

## NATURAL RIGHTS

The principle of natural rights formed the conceptual foundation of the Revolution. It was a core belief of the delegates to the Convention. In his June 27 remarks, Luther Martin noted, "[T]he first principle of government is founded on the natural rights of individuals . . . Nor can any state demand a surrender of any of those rights."[60]

The Committee on Detail referred to natural rights on July 23. "Since we are not working on the natural rights of men not yet gathered into society, but upon those rights modified by society and interwoven with what we call the rights of states."[61]

On September 12, it was moved and seconded to appoint a Committee to prepare a bill of rights. The motion failed unanimously.[62] Roger Sherman suggested the reason for omitting a bill of rights within the Constitution on September 12: "Mr. Sherman was for securing the rights of the people where requisite. The State Declarations of Rights are not repealed by this Constitution; and being in force are sufficient . . . The Legislature may be safely trusted."[63]

While the delegates thought securing these rights was redundant, the citizenry did not. On September 15, George Mason lamented that in the final draft "the declaration of Rights, and the laws of the general government being paramount to the laws and Constitutions of the several states, the Declaration of Rights in the separate States are no security."[64] On June 8, 1789, in his first act as a Virginia congressman, Madison remedied this omission. He submitted a draft bill of rights to the First Congress. "The first of these amendments relates to what may be called a bill of rights. I will own that I never considered this provision so essential to the federal constitution, to make it improper to ratify it, until such an amendment was added . . ."[65]

## FEDERALISM

Federalism is one of the delegates' great innovations and forms the basis of the government they constructed: a government built from the bottom up, rather than the top down, with each level doing what it should do best. The debate over its structure permeated the entire Convention. Eldridge Gerry discussed "a distinction between a federal and national government."[66] Wilson said, "[T]he only criterion of determining what is federal and what is national is this, those acts which are for the government of the states are purely federal, those which are for the Government of the Citizens of the individual States are national and not federal."[67] The entire day of August 30 was given over to debating the limits of federalism.[68]

The debate over sovereignty is integral to the principle of federalism and to the workings of divided government. The Framers understood that "states are not sovereign."[69] Wilson stated, "[T]he States were not 'sovereigns' in the sense contended for by some. They did not possess the peculiar features of sovereignty. They could not make war, nor peace, nor alliances, nor treaties."[70] "States were never sovereign," said Elbridge Gerry.[71] Madison also discussed "the limitations on the sovereignty of the States."[72] Said Gerry, "We never were independent states, were not such now, & never could be on the principles of the Confederation."[73]

## RESTRAINTS ON A SINGLE SOURCE OF AUTHORITY

The principle of restraints on a single source of authority resounded throughout the entire Convention. Said Wilson on separation of powers: "[I]n order to controul the Legislative authority, you must divide it."[74] In February 1788, Madison detailed the importance of this principle in Federalist No. 51.

The division of political power between the small and larger states provided virtually the only subject of debate for the first six weeks of the Convention. The "Great Compromise" settled the acrimony: one chamber of the legislature would be chosen on the basis of population, while the states would be equally represented in the second chamber.

On June 6, Madison stated, "[A] check is devised for three purposes—to prevent encroachments by the Legislature on the Executive, the Judicial or on private rights."[75] On June 26, Madison again observed, "[I]t will be proper to take a view of the ends to be served by it. These were first to protect the people against their rulers: secondly, to protect (the people) against the transient impressions which they themselves might be led. . . . An obvious precaution against this danger would be to divide the trust between different bodies of men, who might watch and check each other."[76] And again on July 11, "[T]he truth was that all men having power ought to be distrusted to a certain degree."[77]

The delegates debated whether to create a Privy Council—that is, an advisory council to the president, similar to one that existed in England. Its powers did not flow from the electorate. Although the idea had considerable support, Governeur Morris dispatched the idea in two sentences on September 7: "The question of a council was considered in the Committee [on Style], where it was judged that the President by persuading his council—to concur in the wrong measures, would acquire their protection for them."[78]

Looking back in February 1792, Madison, in a House debate, emphasized, "[T]his is not an indefinite Government, deriving its powers from the general terms prefixed to the specific powers, but a limited government, tied down to the specified powers which explain and define the general terms."[79]

## PUBLIC VIRTUE

The importance of public virtue percolated throughout the summer. The delegates assumed that elected officials would have the same knowledge and experience as they themselves possessed. Said Madison on May 31, "[R]efining the popular appointments by successive filtrations"[80] would ensure that the federal government would contain only the most experienced officials. That was another reason why the Senate would initially be elected by state legislatures. On May 31, Wilson affirmed that the delegates should raise "the federal pyramid to a considerable altitude, and for that reason, wished to give it as broad a base as possible."[81] On July 2, Governeur Morris asked, "[W]hat qualities are necessary to constitute a check in this case? *Abilities* and *virtue*, are equally necessary in both branches."[82]

On July 26, John Dickinson said, "[I]t seemed improper that any man of merit should be subjected to disabilities in the Republic where merit was understood to form the great title to public trust, honors, & rewards."[83]

Finally, as Madison stated in Federalist No. 10, "[A]s each representative will be chosen by a greater number of citizens in the large than in the small republic, it will be more difficult for unworthy candidates to practice with success the vicious arts by which elections are too often carried; and the suffrages of the people being more free, will be more likely to centre in men who possess the most attractive merit and the most diffusive and established characters."[84]

## COMMON LAW

The principle of common law was rarely discussed at the Convention. It seems to have fallen into the same category as natural rights: that is, it was simply taken for granted among the delegates. On August 17, Madison assumed common law was operating.[85] The concept that the judiciary must decide a "case or controversy" (Article III, Section 2, Clause 1) was reinforced by John Rutledge on July 21. "The judges ought never to give their opinion on a law til it comes before them."[86]

Mason's objections to the Constitution in the closing moments of the Convention also underscore the principle of common law. "Nor are the people secured even in the enjoyment of the benefit of the common law (which stands here upon no other foundation than its having been adopted by the respective acts forming the constitutions of the several States.)"[87] Mason felt that what several states had done by explicitly incorporating common law within their state constitutions should also be included in the Federal Constitution itself.

The Seventh Amendment in the Bill of Rights mentions "common law" twice. It explicitly states that the right of trial by jury shall be guaranteed in civil trials "according to the rules of the common law."

## JUDICIAL REVIEW

The principle of judicial review was long assumed by the Constitution's creators. On July 17, Madison noted that the "Court has the right to review state laws."[88] On July 21, Martin added, "And as to the Constitutionality of laws, that point will come before the Judges in their proper official character. In this character they have a negative on the laws."[89]

On July 23, Gouverneur Morris said, "[L]egislative alterations not conformable to the federal compact, would clearly not be valid. The Judges would consider them as null & void."[90] To which Madison added "A law violating a constitution established by the people themselves, would be considered by the Judges null & void."[91]

Lest there be any doubt about the principle of judicial review, John Mercer from Virginia said, "He disapproved of the Doctrine that the Judges as expositors of the Constitution should have authority to declare a law void." The delegates defeated his motion to that end.[92]

## ADVERSARY SYSTEM OF CRIMINAL JUSTICE

As a principle, the adversary system of criminal justice is not clearly stated, but it is reflected in the concern over trial by jury in both criminal and civil cases. On August 27, the Convention provided for trial by jury in criminal cases.[93] The Seventh Amendment extends the right of a jury trial to civil trials.

The adversary system is also suggested in an August 27 debate. Wilson said that the Committee (on Detail) "meant facts as well as law & Common as well as Civil law" in defining the courts' jurisdiction.[94] As Dickinson stated, the delegates added "both as to law & fact" to qualify the Court's appellate jurisdiction.[95] The "Assistance of Counsel" is specifically guaranteed in the Sixth Amendment.

## PRIVATE ORDERING

The principle of private ordering is reflected in Article I, Section 8 against the impairment of contracts, ensuring an individual's right to make his own agreements and having them enforced by the courts. In the Convention itself, Rufus King suggested "a prohibition on the States to interfere in private contracts."[96]

## DIRECT BUT LIMITED GOVERNMENT INVOLVEMENT IN THE ECONOMY

The Constitution gives Congress the general power to regulate commerce but with important exceptions. Said Randolph. "Every one is impressed with the idea of general regulation of commerce. Can Congress do this? And would it not be dangerous to entrust such a body with the power, when they are so dreaded on these grounds?"[97]

On August 28, Sherman reported from the Committee on "regulation of commerce."[98] On August 29, there was a lengthy debate on the commercial powers of Congress.[99] During this debate, Rutledge added, "[I]t did not follow from a grant of the power to regulate trade, that it would be abused."[100] Government's direct but limited role in the economy is written into the Constitution in Article I, Section 8.

The importance of science and technology to the new republic's success is reflected in the government's right to protect intellectual property. It is stated in the Committee Report on September 5— indicating the government's right to grant patents[101]—and formally incorporated in one of the Article I, Section 8 provisions.

## FREE TRADE (FREE MARKETS)

The extensive debate on regulating trade presumes there is commerce to regulate. The existence of free markets and fair competition was a necessary corollary to the government's power to regulate commerce. Again, this debate pervades much of the Convention, couched as how and when the government should intervene in the economy.

## PLURALISM

The principle of pluralism lay at the very heart of Madison's plan for the new republic. On June 6, Madison expressed his vision, which he repeated in Federalist No. 10. "All civilized societies would be divided into different Sects, Factions & interests . . . In all cases where a majority are united by a common interest or passion, the rights of the minority are in danger . . . The only remedy is to enlarge the sphere, & thereby divide the community into so great a number of interests & parties, that in the 1st place a majority will not be likely at the same moment to have a common interest separate from that of the whole or the minority; and in the 2d place, that they should have such an interest, they may not be able to unite in the pursuit of it. It was incumbent on us then to try this remedy, and with a view to frame a republican system on such a scale & in such form as will controul all the evils which have been experienced."[102]

Madison hoped that a common good would arise out of the competition between competing factions. Again in Federalist No. 10, Madison wrote

[I]t clearly appears, that the same advantage which a republic has over a democracy, in controlling the effects of faction, is enjoyed by a large over a small republic . . . Does the advantage consist in the substitution of representatives whose enlightened views and virtuous sentiments render them superior to local prejudices and schemes of injustice? It will not be denied that the representation of the Union will be most likely to possess these requisite endowments. Does it consist in the greater security afforded by a greater variety of parties, against the event of any one party being able to outnumber and oppress the rest? In an equal degree does the increased variety of parties comprised within the Union, increase this security.[103]

Preventing specific interest groups and wealthy individuals from directly incorporating themselves into the government was implicit in the delegates' principle of pluralism. Dickenson "doubted the policy of interweaving into a Republican constitution a veneration for wealth. He had always understood that a veneration for poverty & virtue, were the objects of Republican encouragement."[104]

The general respect the delegates had for early policies of open immigration was also evident at the Convention. On August 13, Madison said that he "wished to invite foreigners of merit & republican principles among us. America was indebted to emigration for her settlement & Prosperity. That part of America which had encouraged them most had advanced most rapidly in population, agriculture & the arts."[105]

## EQUALITARIAN SOCIETY

The principle of an equalitarian society was one of the foundations of a republican society, though the delegates were less than inclusive on which groups was covered. On June 25, Charles Pinckney stated, "[T] he people of the U. States are perhaps the most singular of any we are acquainted with. Among them are fewer distinctions of fortune and less of rank, than among the inhabitants of any other nation. Every freeman has the right to the same protection & security; . . . Every member of Society, almost, will enjoy an equal power of arriving at the Supreme offices . . . None will be excluded by birth, & few by fortune."[106]

But there was certainly concern for losing that "equality of condition."[107] As Madison acknowledged on June 26, "[I]n framing a system which we wish to last for ages, we should not lose sight of the changes that ages will produce. An increase of population will of necessity increase the proportion of those who will labour under all the hardships of life, & secretly design for a more equal distribution of its blessings."[108] The delegates were equally concerned about the conditions these changes would produce. Said Madison, "[T]he man who is possessed of wealth, who lolls on his sofa or rolls in his carriage, cannot judge of the wants or feelings of the day laborer."[109]

The moral, political, and economic dimensions of slavery were well understood and provided a constant point of friction among the delegates. The examples are many—notable among them is a lengthy debate on August 22 in which seventeen delegates participated.[110] In the end, the delegates opted for union over slavery. The consequences of that decision have played out over the Republic's history.

## SEPARATION OF CHURCH AND STATE

The principle of religious freedom and the separation of church and state was never questioned by the delegates. Pinckney noted on June 25, "[O]ur true situation appears to be this—a new extensive country containing within itself all the materials for forming a government capable of extending to its citizens all the blessings of civil & religious liberty—capable of making them happy at home."[111]

The delegates were clearly uneasy with Washington's June 8 motion for a daily prayer. They adjourned without voting on this.[112] And on August 23 a resolution that "no religious test shall be required as a qualification to any office or public trust under the authority of the United States" passed unanimously.[113]

In his lengthy report in November 1787 to the Maryland State

Legislature on the Philadelphia Convention, Martin recalled that "no religious test shall be required as a qualification to any office or public trusts under the United States was adopted by a great majority of the convention, and without much debate."[114] The principle of separation of church and state was formally incorporated in the First Amendment, which states, "Congress shall make no law respecting an establishment of religion, or prohibiting the free exercise thereof . . ."

## NATIONAL SECURITY

The principle of national security was clearly voiced at the Convention. As the Preamble states, the delegates intended "to insure domestic Tranquility, [and] provide for the common defence."[115] Protection from overseas threats and domestic violence was another major theme of the Convention. On May 30, Gerry said, "[S]tates in their appointments point directly to a government capable of 'the common defense, security of liberty and general welfare.'"[116] On May 31, Sherman lists "the object of the Union: 1. defence against foreign danger. 2. against internal disputes & a resort to force. 3. Treaties with foreign nations . . ."[117] And on June 6, Madison himself said, "[T]he primary objects of civil society are the security of property and public safety."[118]

That there were limits to this principle is equally clear. Foreshadowing Eisenhower's concerns 175 years later, on August 18 Gerry worried that "there was no check here against standing armies in time of peace."[119] Said Madison on August 23, "[T]he greatest danger to liberty is from large standing armies."[120]

1. James Madison, August 1786. As cited in David O. Stewart, *The Summer of 1787: The Men Who Invented the Constitution* (New York: Simon & Schuster, 2008), p. 9.

2. James Madison, *Notes of Debates in the Federal Convention of 1787, Reported by James Madison*, Introduction by Adrienne Koch (Athens, OH: Ohio University Press, 1966).

3. The Declaration of Independence (1776).

4. William Penn, in his *Preface to the First Frame of Government for Pennsylvania*, which was formally adopted in England, April 25, 1682. The William Penn Tercentenary Committee, *Remember William Penn*, 2nd ed. (Commonwealth of Pennsylvania, 1945), p. 81.

5. Tip O'Neill, cited in Robert H. Bremmer, *American Philanthropy* (Chicago: University of Chicago Press, 1966), p. 201.

6. Abraham Lincoln, the Gettysburg Address, November 1863.

7. Richard Beeman, private e-mail, May 15, 2011.

8. Robert Pear, "In House, Many Spoke with One Voice: Lobbyists," *New York Times*, November 15, 2009.

9. Madison et al., *The Federalist Papers*, Federalist No. 10, pp. 77–84.

10. Ibid.

11. These Supreme Court decisions were made in a series of cases including *National League of Cities v. Usery*, 426 U.S. 833 (1976), which was overruled by *Garcia v. San Antonio Metropolitan Transit Authority*, 469 U.S. 528 (1985).

12. Elbridge Gerry, *Notes to the Federal Convention,* June 6, 1787. In Ralph Ketcham, *The Anti-Federalist Papers and the Constitutional Convention Debates* (New York: Signet Classics, 2003).

13. Brannon Denning, private e-mail, November 1, 2011.

14. Anthony Lewis, cited in Henry J. Abraham, "Effectiveness of Governmental Operations, The Annals of the American Political and Social Science," *Annals,* 426, July 1976, American Academy of Political and Social Science, p. 81.

15. John Hart Ely, *Democracy and Distrust: A Theory of Judicial Review* (Cambridge, Mass.: Harvard University Press, 1980).

16. *Gideon v. Wainwright,* 372 U.S. 335, 345 (1963).

17. Henry M. Hart, Jr., and Albert M. Sacks, "The Legal Process: Basic Problems in the Making and Application of Law" (tentative edition, 1958).

18. Ibid., 1958, pp. 110–169.

19. Letter from James Madison to Thomas Jefferson (1786), in Philip B. Kurland and Ralph Lerner, *The Founders' Constitution* (Chicago: The University of Chicago Press, 1986).

20. Ralph Louis Ketcham, *James Madison: A Biography* (Newtown, Conn.: American Political Biography Press, 2003), p. 636.

21. Charles Austin Beard, *An Economic Interpretation of the Constitution of the United States* (New York: Macmillan, 1921).

22. Alexis de Tocqueville, *Democracy in America, A New Translation* by George Lawrence, Edited by J. P. Mayer (New York: Anchor Books, 1969).

23. *McCulloch v. Maryland,* 17 U.S. 316, 421 (1819).

24. Pelatiah Webster (1791), quoted in Max Seville, *Seeds of Liberty* (Seattle, Wash.: University of Washington Press, 1948), p. 211.

25. Dan Schwartz, *The Future of Finance: How Private Equity and Venture Capital Will Shape the Global Economy* (Hoboken, N.J.: Wiley, 2010).

26. Madison, *Notes of Debates,* pp. 75–77.

27. Ibid., pp. 375–376.

28. Ketcham, *James Madison: A Biography* (Newtown, Conn.: American Political Biography Press, 1971), p. 201.

29. Madison, *Notes of Debates,* pp. 375–76.

30. Madison, *Notes of Debates,* pp. 543–545.

31. Margaret Mead, *And Keep Your Powder Dry: An Anthropologist Looks at America* (New York: Morrow, 1942).

32. Frederic Jackson Turner, *The Significance of the Frontier in American History,* a paper read at the meeting of the American Historical Association in Chicago, July 12, 1893, during the World Columbian Exposition.

33. Louis Hartz, *The Liberal Tradition in America* (New York: Harcourt, Brace & World, 1955).

34. David Potter, *People of Plenty: Economic Abundance and the American Character* (Chicago: University of Chicago Press, 1954).

35. Alexander Hamilton, James Madison, and John Jay, *The Federalist Papers* (New York: The New American Library of World Literature, Inc., 1961).

36. Gordon Wood, *The Creation of the American Republic, 1776–1787* (Chapel Hill, N.C.: University of North Carolina Press, 1969).

37. Measures implemented under President Franklin Roosevelt included the Emergency Banking Relief Act, which provided for reopening of sound banks; the federal Emergency Relief Administration, which provided funds for states to relieve unemployment; the Agricultural Adjustment Act, which was the beginning of farm subsidies; the federal Housing Administration Act, which encouraged monthly mortgage payments; the Tennessee Valley Development Act, which created an independent public corporation to revitalize the region; the National Industrial Recovery Act, which called upon industry groups to regulate hours and wages; and the Public Works Administration, which put many Americans back to work building public works projects. Finally, the Social Security Act of 1935 authorized payroll taxes and gave the Social Security Board the right to administer unemployment compensation and old-age benefits. The Wagner Act of 1935 created the National Labor Relations Board to oversee union elections.

38. *Brown v. Board of Education of Topeka*, 347 U.S. 483 (1954).

39. Mead, *And Keep Your Powder Dry*, p. 37.

40. Ketcham, *James Madison: A Biography*, pp. 165, 167.

41. James Madison, *Memorial and Remonstrance Against Religious Assessments* (1785).

42. *Everson v. Board of Education*, 330 U.S. 1 (1947).

43. Edmond Nathaniel Cahn and Lenore L. Cahn, *Confronting Injustice: The Edmond Cahn reader* (Essay index reprint series) (Boston: Little, Brown and Company, 1962, 1965), p. 179.

44. Cahn and Cahn, *Confronting Injustice.*

45. Ibid, p. 183.

46. *Everson v. Board of Education*, 330 U.S. 1 (1947).

47. *Marsh v. Chambers*, 463 U.S. 783 (1983), Chief Justice Warren Burger's majority opinion.

48. Ketcham, *James Madison: A Biography*, p. 471.

49. Dwight D. Eisenhower, Farewell Address to the Nation, January 17, 1961.

50. The Center for Arms Control and Non-Proliferation. http://armscontrolcenter.org/policy/securityspending/articles/FY_2012_House_Defense_Approps_Committee/; "Federal Government Outlays by Function and Subfunction: 1962–2015 Fiscal Year 2011 (Table 3.2)"; The China Post, http://www.chinapost.com.tw/taiwan/national/national-news/2011/03/08/293792/p2/Military-budget.htm; Defense News, http://www.defensenews.com/story.php?i=5016720.

51. Henry Kissinger, *Does America Need a Foreign Policy? Toward a Diplomacy for the 21st Century* (New York: Simon & Schuster, 2001).

52. Max G. Manwaring (Ed.), *Papers from the Conference on Homeland Protection* (Strategic Studies Institute, October 2000), p. 263.

53. U.S. Treasury Department, *Financial Regulatory Reform: A New Foundation*, June 17, 2009.

54. Center for Responsive Politics, http://www.opensecrets.org/lobby/index.php

55. Max Farrand (Ed.), *The Records of the Federal Convention of 1787*, 4 volumes, revised edition (New Haven, Conn.: Yale University Press, 1937, reprinted 1966), vol. 1, p. 451.

56. Ibid., vol. 1, p. 132.

57. Ibid., vol. 2, p. 88.

58. Ibid., vol. 1, p. 440.

59. Ibid., vol. 2, p. 476.

60. Ibid., vol. 1, p. 440.

61. Ibid., vol. 2, p. 137.

62. Ibid., vol. 2, p. 588.

63. Ibid., vol. 2, p. 588.

64. Ibid., vol. 2, p. 637.

65. Ibid., vol. 3, p. 357.

66. Ibid., vol. 1, p. 42.

67. Ibid., vol. 1, pp. 331–332.

68. Ibid., vol. 2, pp. 461–467.

69. Ibid., vol. 1, p. 98.

70. Ibid., vol. 1, p. 323.

71. Ibid., vol. 1, p. 467.

72. Ibid., vol. 1, p. 464.

73. Ibid., vol. 1, p. 467.

74. Ibid., vol. 1, p. 254.

75. Ibid., vol. 1, p. 144.

76. Ibid., vol. 1, p. 421.

77. Ibid., vol. 1, p. 584

78. Ibid., vol. 2, p. 542.

79. Ibid., vol. 3, p. 366.

80. Madison, *Notes of Debates*, p. 40.

81. Farrand, vol. 1, p. 43.

82. Ibid., vol. 1, p. 512.

83. Ibid., vol. 2, p. 123.

84. Madison et al., *The Federalist Papers*, Federalist No. 10, pp. 77–84.

85. Madison, *Notes of Debates*, pp. 473–74.

86. Farrand, vol. 2, p. 80.

87. Ibid., vol. 2, p. 637.

88. Madison, *Notes of Debates*, p. 304.

89. Farrand, vol. 2, p. 76.

90. Ibid., vol. 2, p. 92.

91. Ibid., vol. 2, p. 93.

92. Ibid., vol. 2, p. 298.

93. Ibid., vol. 2, p. 433.

94. Ibid., vol. 2, p. 431.

95. Ibid., vol. 2, p. 431.

96. Ibid., vol. 2, p. 439.

97. Ibid., vol. 1, p. 263.

98. Ibid., vol. 2, p. 437.

99. Ibid., vol. 2, pp. 449–455.

100. Ibid., vol. 2, p. 452.

100. Ibid., vol. 2, p. 452.

101. Ibid., vol. 2, p. 505.

102. Ibid., vol. 1, p. 136.

103. Madison et al., *The Federalist Papers*, Federalist No. 10, p. 77.

104. Farrand, vol. 2, p. 123.

105. Ibid., vol. 2, p. 268.

106. Ibid., vol. 1, pp. 398, 400.

107. Ibid., vol. 1, p. 400.

108. Ibid., vol. 1, p. 422.

109. Ibid., vol. 1, p. 431.

110. Ibid., vol. 2, pp. 369–375.

111. Ibid., vol. 1, p. 402.

112. Ibid., vol. 1, p. 452.

113. Ibid., vol. 2, p. 61.

114. Ibid., vol. 3, p. 227.

115. *The Constitution of the United States*, Preamble.

116. Farrand, vol. 1, p. 43.

117. Ibid., vol. 1, p. 133.

118. Ibid., vol. 1, p. 147.

119. Ibid., vol. 2, p. 329.

120. Ibid., vol. 2, p. 388.

www.ingramcontent.com/pod-product-compliance
Lightning Source LLC
Chambersburg PA
CBHW050535280326
41933CB00011B/1598